The Pursuit of Self Improvement

Books 1-4

JESSICA MARKS

Contents

BOOK 1: TIME MANAGEMENT FOR ENTREPRENEURS

Are You Ready For Change?

Congratulations!

As you are reading this, I'm assuming that you're already running your own business or you are very interested in making that leap in the near future.

Many dream about ditching the 9 to 5 grind and going into business for themselves. Not everyone has the confidence to make such a major change, but for those that do, it can mean a new level of freedom that can change one's life significantly.

I know what that freedom feels like because I'm fulfilling a lifelong dream of location independence while currently living in Thailand.

Running my own business from home, or more accurately in my case, from anywhere in the world, has been a massive achievement for me and I want YOU to feel that level of success for yourself as well.

Regardless if your dream is to be able to work from anywhere in the world or to work from your own office chair in your own home so that you can enjoy a higher quality of life with your family, the common theme for ditching the regular J-O-B is similar.

For most people entrepreneurship and working from home means a massive increase in personal freedom.

Having been there myself and also knowing many entrepreneurs and the common issues we all face, I know how critical it can be to get going as fast as you can with a good habit of time management and high productivity. I know how easy it can be for procrastination and poor time management to get the best of us if we aren't prepared.

The Problem

A contributing factor as to why some otherwise passionate entrepreneurs end up going back to the same 9 to 5's they so desperately wanted to get away from in the first place, is the inability to manage one's time effectively. Poor time management skills and consistent procrastination can lead to missed opportunities, profit loss and eventually business failure if one isn't careful.

While most go about taking great care to set up the business side of things, very few take into consideration the pros and cons of working from home. Sometimes the lure of being the master of one's own time overshadows some of the realities associated with working from home.

Office Time vs Home Time

There are a lot more "controls" in place when working in an office or other business environment. For instance, your co-worker's five year old isn't allowed to run, jump and disturb others in the office setting.

If you have young children at home, it can be challenging trying to work while at the same time allowing your children to enjoy their home environment. They don't understand that it's not "play time" all the time because you're home. How do you handle that? How do you schedule time for family and your business?

Too Much Time Can Be A Problem Too

It's ironic. The most popular reasons people decide to work from home are to make more money, to have more time to travel, to spend time with family and to just do the things they've always wanted to do.

Instead, often time becomes something work from home entrepreneurs end up chasing like a carrot on a stick!

Why is that?

Well, when you work for an employer, your time belongs to your employer and they never let you forget it. Your boss decides when you arrive to work, what time you can go to lunch, what must be done by a certain time and when you get to go home.

But when you choose to work for yourself, suddenly you, and you alone, are responsible for how that time is spent. There's no one around telling you when to do this, that and the other. You end up enjoying your freedom so much that before you realize it, you've spent much of the day getting very little done at all.

If you don't learn some time management skills and use them daily, you'll find yourself stressed out and "out" of business!

The Solution

That is where this book comes in! I've put together all of the best methods I know of to help create an environment for massive productivity.

If you're struggling to keep your head above water and your work from home dream has become a nightmare because you can't seem to get anything done, now is NOT the time to feel sorry for yourself and just give up!

I've been where you are right now. I know what it feels like to be overwhelmed and disorganized, but working from home doesn't have to be a nightmare when you have the right strategies and systems in place to keep you on track and focused.

If I could show you some simple but very effective ways to manage your time and increase your productivity would you be interested?

Imagine this:

You no longer spend the majority of your time working and accomplishing very little. Instead, you are able to get things done and in less time than before.

Missing deadlines becomes a thing of the past because you have a new system that makes it almost impossible to miss those important dates.

You lead a less stressful healthier life that allows you to have balance. That means you're able to run your business successfully and still enjoy time with family and friends.

You're able to grow your business because you understand the importance of leveraging time and it has a positive impact on the growth of your business.

Procrastination is no longer a problem and this allows you to boost your productivity like never before!

That's just the tip of the iceberg when it comes to time management issues for work from home entrepreneurs.

Did you know that a cluttered work environment can stop your productivity dead in its tracks?

I'll show you how to stop distractions like email and Facebook from robbing you of valuable time.

If you're having problems finishing tasks each day and still feeling run down, your diet could be ruining your business!

Running your own business, especially from home, has a lot of unique challenges, but if you're ready to put in the effort and be consistent, the strategies you are about to learn will allow you to enjoy the benefits listed above and a lot more.

How To Use This Book

It's not necessary to read this guide in any particular order.

The guide is presented in a logical sequence beginning with what are the three main foundational elements for the process of getting yourself organized.

You can also go straight to the section or sections that you feel you need the most help with.

Each chapter is divided into smaller sub-sections and you can view the Table of Contents to go directly to the sections that interest you the most.

Let's get started!

FOUNDATION #1:
Organizing Your Mental Space

Organizing Your Mental Space

Before you can get a real hold on managing your time for success, you need to take some preliminary steps first. You've made the decision to branch out on your own to start and run your business from home. That presents a lot of challenges.

When you decide to go solo it means taking control of your time. Once the excitement begins to wear off, the reality sets in and you realize you now have to answer to yourself. If you fail to get something done and it ends up costing you money, there's no big corporate entity around to absorb some of the costs.

It's all on you.

That's a lot of pressure! So it's so important to make sure you don't end up self-sabotaging yourself and your business. When the pressure is on, you're more likely to make mistakes that can cause you to waste valuable time which can negatively affect your bottom line. I don't think I have to tell you the mental roller coaster you'll find yourself on when you're uncertain about your finances! It then becomes a battle of your mind to keep it all together.

In this section, we're going to begin with the foundation of gaining clarity about your business and everything that you want to achieve so that when you find yourself getting off track with the time management and production, you have something concrete to go back to.

Clarity Is Key

I know what it's like to feel overwhelmed, especially at the start of your business endeavors.

Regardless of where you are at, if you are feeling that sense of overwhelm, I suggest you set aside some time to really gain some clarity about your business, your hopes for your future, your goals…basically everything that has to do with your reasons for making the decision to go into business for yourself.

Schedule some quiet time that is very specifically set aside for this purpose. Perhaps you can think of it as a little retreat for your business…even if the only one attending is you. You, as CEO, are the key person in your business. Have paper and pencil handy so that you can really get some things on paper that will help you to gain the clarity that you need to succeed.

Let's get started!

Know Your "Why" For Your Business

This may seem like a simple step, but I think it really helps to think about (and write down) all of the reminders as to why you've decided to be in business for yourself. If you've recently left a job you don't like this will be easy for you. Remind yourself of all the reasons you want to make your business work

For many of us, the main reasons have to do with income and time freedom.

Working for yourself can mean that the sky is the limit when it comes to how much money you are able to make. Your income can be a direct correlation to the amount of smart time and effort you put into your business.

This is motivation enough for most people to discover ways to succeed as quickly as possible.

Of course there are other benefits to working for yourself. If you are a parent, a valid reason might be that you want to be able to spend more time at home with your children. Running your own schedule can allow you to have the time flexibility that you never could have had while working for someone else.

List all of your big "whys" for starting your business. Hopefully this exercise will leave you feeling extremely motivated!

Your Vision/Mission Statement

During your clarity session regarding your business, it would be a good idea to start creating a mission statement and vision for your particular business.

Regardless of what stage you are at or what it is that you are doing, you will have more success if you treat it as a business from the very beginning. Crafting a mission statement that describes why your business exists will lay a great foundation for that attitude. Writing the perfect mission and vision statements goes beyond the scope of this book, but a simple search online will bring a lot of information and examples for how to go about this.

Here is an article about writing a good mission statement.
http://www.entrepreneur.com/article/65230

Here is an article about writing a good vision statement.
http://www.businessnewsdaily.com/3882-vision-statement.html

Your Ideal Day

These exercises are all in preparation to get you in the frame of mind for being ready to commit 100% to the success of your business, so no matter how silly the exercise might seem, please do give it a try.

Here, I want you to picture and write out your ideal work day. This may or may not include actually having to be sitting at your desk working away on your computer. Perhaps your ideal work day includes a hammock on a beach somewhere sipping a drink with an umbrella in it. Maybe your ideal day means that you have complete financial freedom to be able to pick and choose the elements of your business that you actually want to work at on a daily basis, passing the other items off to a virtual assistant or multiple employees.

Please do not hold back here…the sky is the limit and this is not the time to stifle your dreams. We want to put everything out there and then when we get to our goal setting section, we will pull in the reigns a bit to set out a realistic plan for moving forward with your dreams.

You have to start somewhere and it is critical to know what it is that you are aiming for.

Your Goals

A big part of getting yourself organized mentally includes knowing where it is you want to go (the vision you have for your business) and then building a concrete plan as to how you will achieve that ultimate aim.

Goal setting is a big part of the success of a business and it will be one of the essential elements moving forward as you really get a handle on good time management and productivity strategies.

Begin by looking forward at least 3-5 years down the road for your business. What are the major goals and milestones that you would like to be hitting? These can be financial goals as well as other goals that show the growth of your business. Your goals should be clear and concise.

Let's use the example of someone who is a writer just beginning their self-publishing process.

An example of some 3 year goals might be:

*to have 8 novels published
*to have 20 short stories published
*to have a FaceBook following of 10,000 fans
*to have 10,000 followers on Twitter
*to have 5,000 email subscribers
*to be making $100,000/year from my writing

And then you would break it down further...

An example of some 1 year goals might be:

*to have 2 novels published
*to have 5 short stories published
*to have a FaceBook following of 3,000 fans
*to have 3,000 followers on Twitter
*to have 1,000 email subscribers
*to be making $20,000/year from my writing

Note that for the 1 year goals in this case, I do not break them down according to 1/3 of the 3 year goals because I believe that there would be a bit of a learning curve in year 1. Once there would be some momentum going (as is often the case with new authors), years 2 and 3 would pick up a lot in terms of learning and production.

And then you would further break those 1 year goals down into quarterly and monthly goals.

Your month 1 goals might look something like this based on our example:

*plot/outline novel #1
*decide on the genre for the short stories and if they will be stand alone or part of a series
*create a Facebook page: follow 10 other pages per wk and make 4-6 posts per week.
*create a Twitter account: follow 10 accounts each day and tweet or schedule at least 1 tweet per day
*research and choose an email service for list building
*open a business bank account and create spreadsheets for tracking business income and expenses

From here, you can plot out weekly goals and then your daily task/to-do list.

Your goals will reflect your own business whether it is something totally independent as is the case of a writer, or a business that is service related. If your business is dependent on clients, your goals would reflect certain milestones regarding new client acquisition and your tasks to get there would reflect the things that you can do to find and recruit new clients for your business.

Have fun with this! This should leave you with a great feeling of clarity and the motivation to go forward on a daily basis to achieve your goals.

Developing The Right Mindset

Have you ever noticed that when your environment is a mess it usually correlates to whatever is going on in your life? It's more common than you may realize. If you're worried about finances, getting more clients, paying the bills and taking care of your family, you're going to have a hard time trying to stay organized.

Step 1

Write down any fears or doubts you have about running your business, family issues etc...

Listen, you've got to be honest with yourself. No sugar coating anything! The whole of this exercise is to "air" out what issues may impede your ability to run your business either now or in the future. When your mind is constantly focusing on "problems" it robs you of time. Instead of taking care of business, you end up wasting time worrying and thinking about all the worst possible outcomes that could possibly happen.

That's a colossal waste of time!

So get your pen and paper and write down those thoughts that get in the way of your ability to be productive. If you're having a hard time trying to come up with things, think of it this way.

What keeps you up at night?

The answers to that question are the fears and doubts you need to start writing down.

Step 2

Now read each one out loud. Often when you verbalize something and hear the sound of your own voice it forces both your conscious and subconscious mind to sit up and take notice. It will be a bit uncomfortable at first but don't skip this part.

Step 3

The majority of stuff that we worry about in our lives can be solved on some level. The key is to focus on the things that you can control and allow yourself to accept what you cannot control, but acknowledge that the problem exists.

Step 4

Take each issue and write a possible solution or possible outcome for each. Write whatever comes to mind even if it seems crazy. When you write without focusing on "getting it right" you allow more thoughts to flow freely. That's when you'll have your "aha moment" and begin to see the possibilities for fixing various issues.

Step 5

Now read your new solutions out loud. Now you're forcing your conscious and subconscious mind to pay attention to this new information. Keep repeating the solutions you've come up with over and over again. The more you hear yourself reciting a better outcome, the sooner you'll begin to believe you can find the answers you need. This means you'll end up spending less time worrying about things you already know you can work out on some level.

In order for this technique to work, you'll need to practice on a regular basis. Each time a new "worry" pops up in your mind, deal with it right then and there! The more you do this, the quicker you can get rid of thoughts that steal valuable time from you throughout your day.

Now let's move on to tackling your work space.

FOUNDATION #2:
Organizing Your Physical Space

The Importance Of Your Organized Work Space

In the last section, we went over the importance of organizing your "head space" for what you are wanting to accomplish with your business.

Here we are going to talk about another important foundational principle to good time management and productivity and that is having a physical work environment that best suits your needs and is pleasant to work in.

It is very difficult to engage in good productivity strategies when your home office is disorganized and cluttered. For many people, a cluttered desk and work space is likely to carry over into a cluttered mind and this is what we do not want.

Contrary to this, there is something about a very organized work space that automatically puts one in the mental zone of being productive and very clear about the tasks that need to happen.

In this section, I'm going to help you to create a friendly productive work environment that I believe will set the tone for your new and improved productive work zone!

Organizing Your Physical Space

You'll accomplish a lot more during your work day if you organize your work area first. Clutter is a huge time stealer. When you have to spend time looking for that important client file, your cell phone and a long list of other things over and over again, you're wasting time. Keeping your work space clean and organized virtually eliminates unnecessary time wasting.

Step 1

Choose an area of your home that will be your own personal work space. Ideally you want to choose a room with a door in the quietest part of your home if possible. If you have children or a small home or apartment this may be more of a challenge. Wherever you choose, it should be off limits to anyone not associated with your business. In other words, it's extremely important to establish and clearly explain to other family members that this is your work zone.

Step 2

Once you've established an area, the next step is to furnish it accordingly. This is really important in terms of time management. Choosing the right desk, chair and even your computer set-up all play a role in helping you to use your time more efficiently. Think about it. When you're comfortable don't you perform better? This is especially true if you've got to focus on a big project of some sort. The last thing you want to have to deal with is a nagging backache from sitting hunched over your desk for hours at a time. Pain can be a major distraction.

So you want to choose furniture that will allow you to work comfortably but not so comfortable that you end up snoozing! Try visiting a few different office supply stores so that you can see different kinds of furniture before you buy. This is especially important when choosing a good chair.

I can't stress the importance of getting a high quality ergonomic chair enough. Yes, they can be a bit expensive, but if you'll be spending several hours a day sitting at your desk, do yourself a favor and buy the best you can afford. Your back will thank you later!

Step 3

Next, you'll want to invest in a good storage system. The easiest way to do this may be to look for pre-built office storage systems. This way you won't have to try and visualize what you may need. The work from home entrepreneur boom has prompted several designers to create home office storage units. You can find home office set ups from the very small home office to large scale offices. One of my favorite places to get great storage at reasonable prices is IKEA. Even if you don't care for IKEA, you can get some great ideas by just looking at some of the room displays they create. It's amazing what they can create with some of the smallest of spaces.

It's a good idea to surround yourself with pictures of family and friends. If you will be meeting clients in your home office, don't go overboard.

Adding motivational quotes and pictures to hang on the wall is also a great idea. Whatever keeps you motivated without distracting you from your work is fine and optimal.

A Word About Being "Too Comfortable"

It's important to have a work environment that is both functional and comfortable, but not too comfy. Make sure you're not creating a "second bedroom" atmosphere to the point that you might find yourself drifting off to sleep.

You need to make sure you're able to work comfortably so that you're able to get work done.

Tips

1. Get The Right Chair

Invest in an ergonomic chair that allows you to sit in a way that doesn't compromise your back.

2. Additional Seating

If you have the space, add a more comfortable chair to sit in when you're taking a break or to reward yourself for completing a project, following up with clients, getting your marketing done etc.

3. Dress Code

Although you're working from home and you could work in your pajamas all day, don't! Consider dressing for work just as you did when you worked your 9 to 5. If you were expected to wear business attire, do the same working from home. There's a psychological reason for doing so. Think of this way…in a corporate environment there is often a dress code in place. Doing so helps to create a "look" and may also reinforce the look of professionalism to clients.

It also puts employees in a certain frame of mind. Wearing a suit or business attire means you're there to take care of business. On the other hand, jeans and a sweatshirt is perceived to be less serious and not quite as professional. Of course there are plenty of corporations without dress codes and stress wearing whatever you want within reason.

The point I'm trying to get across to you is to wear clothing in your home office that means "work time" to you. If that means a suit and tie or a blouse and skirt, then wear it. You would be surprised at how your approach to getting things done changes when you "feel" like you're working in a office environment even if that office is an extra room in your home.

Of course, if you can work and be productive in your PJs or sweats, by all means carry on! This is one of the perks of working from home, right?

First Impressions

If an aspect of your home business involves meeting with clients, this is another thing to consider when it comes to how you want to be perceived. Work attire and presenting the right impression is vital to getting and maintaining clients. Unfortunately, people really do judge a book by its cover. So make sure "your cover" is appropriate.

FOUNDATION #3:
Organizing Your Digital Space

Choosing Your Key Work Tools

We now live in an amazing time where digital management tools will be essential for your business. Never before has it been so easy to be connected across multiple devices and be able to take your work with you on the road at a moment's notice.

Depending on your budget, what you currently have and use and how much you plan on working out of a home office will determine what, if any, additional tech gadgets or programs you want to add to your daily routine.

Main Computer

For many people this will be either a desktop computer or a laptop. If your intention is to have a home office and you are also running some hefty programs, then you are sure to need some type of a home computer set-up. This would seem ideal for businesses that utilize graphics and photography services. You probably would not get what you need from using just your laptop computer in terms of screen size. (However, it is easy enough to have additional monitors set up, if your main computer is a laptop).

If your business tends to be more mobile in nature, then a laptop computer is going to make the most sense for you. Many people who mainly work out of their home choose to ultimately have both a desktop and laptop computer for when they are on the go or working away from home.

Tablet Computers/iPads

These lightweight devices have become very popular lately. It's unlikely that you could run your business off of an iPad or tablet for long periods of time, but for certain types of business, these are perfect for mobile work. You can easily do your research, conduct business calls, check e-mail and even write your latest novel all from your iPad. I would consider this more of a luxury addition, rather than something one would choose over a laptop.

Smartphones

Smartphones have changed the way that many people do business today. You can be connected literally almost anywhere in the world via your smartphone. (Note that you have additional costs or things to consider when traveling overseas, but it many cases this is very easy.)

You can do pretty much anything from your smartphone that you could do with your tablet or iPad plus have your phone line for calls and texting.

Organizing Your Computer Files

You can waste a lot of valuable time looking for client projects, documents, billing, correspondence etc. stored on your computer. It's great having all of that hard drive space on your computer right? That is until you can't find what you're looking for.

Here are some tried and true tips for keeping your computer organized.

Consider Having Two Computers

It doesn't matter if you use a Windows based PC or a Mac, consider having two separate computers. You can have one for work and one for personal use. It will make your life so much easier. Plus, there may also be tax advantages as well so be sure to consult with your accountant.

Keeping your business files on a separate PC is another way to stay focused and manage your time better. Instead of wading through files of family pictures mixed in with spreadsheets for your business, you'll be able to keep track of important files and retrieve them much faster. Also, if you keep sensitive client data on your computer you should absolutely not store that data on a personal use computer.

Keep Files Organized With Libraries on Windows 7 & 8

Have you ever noticed the "libraries" section on your Windows PC? Click your start icon and click on Computer. A window will pop up and on the left side of that window you will see the word LIBRARIES.

Basically you can store different files in your library without moving them from their current location. By default Windows has four libraries.

Documents
Music
Pictures
Video

You can also add your own additional folders as well.

How to Use Libraries

Step 1
Go to Libraries from Windows Explorer (See above to do this). Look for a folder our files that are not included in your libraries already. For example, anything that is currently storied on your desktop. Single click to select that folder or file.

Step 2
When you select the folder or file as in step 1, you should now see an option to "Include in library" in the toolbar (above your file list). Now you can choose one of your libraries from that list. For this example just click "Documents."

That's it!

In that same box you will also see the option to "create new library." You can create separate libraries for different parts of your business. This will save you a lot of time because you won't have to remember where you placed a specific file. Instead, you'll just navigate to the appropriate library folder and click.

Remember, Windows does not move the original folder. Libraries just creates an additional location so you can find files a lot quicker.

You can go here to find out more about libraries and view some videos about the process described above.

http://windows.microsoft.com/en-us/windows7/products/features/libraries

Create A Simple Filing System

If you're not interested in utilizing the Library system on your PC you can also create your own system.

The easiest way to keep your files in order is to do so right from the start. That means sitting down before you launch your business and creating basic folders. Now, if you're already in business and you need a GPS device to navigate through your computer's hard drive you can use this system too. It will take some time to get everything reorganized, but the effort will be well worth it when it comes to your ongoing efficiency.

Step 1

Create categories. These will be your folders. Here are a few examples:

Billing
Client Files
Website
Marketing
Advertising

Step 2

Then open each folder and create additional sub-folders. For example:

Billing > Invoices > Due > Paid

Client Files > Projects > Communications

Website > Web Copy > Graphics > Hosting

Marketing > Online > Print

Advertising > Radio > TV

Get the idea? You're simply creating a different folder for different areas of your business.

The sub-folders in each is a way to quickly find very specific files within the main category.

Step 3

Make it a habit to also place new documents specific to each client or other aspects of your business in the appropriate folder every single time. This way you can avoid wasting time trying to remember where you put a client file or information about your website, for example.

Save To Desktop

You may want to save your category folders directly to your desktop. You will be able to locate files much faster this way.

Organizing Mac Files

The Label function on Macs is easy to use, visually cool and will save you a lot of time.

Step 1

Go to Finder > File > Preferences. From there, click on Labels. Look at the top of the Find Preferences window to find the Labels tab.

Step 2

You will see a list of labels already created by default and named by color. Simply change the color name to something business related in each slot.

So, for example, the label named Red could be changed to Contracts. Of course you can name each whatever makes sense for your business.

Do this for as many or as few as you like.

Step 3

Now open any folder on your MAC you want to place under your Contracts label or whatever you've named it.

Right click on a file in that folder and you will see colored boxes. Since, in my example, we made Red = Contracts, we'll select the red box.

That's it you're done!

Repeat the steps for additional files.

The important thing is that you figure out a filing/labeling system that works for you.

Consistency will be the key!

Syncing And Back-Up

Once you have all of your tools chosen, one of the things that you will be thinking about is how to best transfer your information from one device to another.

There are many programs that can make this a very streamlined process for you and you no longer have to worry about transferring information via hard drive or, even more ancient, on to discs.

Evernote is a program that I love that syncs across all devices - use it to compile all kinds of information that you can have at your fingertips regardless of the device you are on.

Evernote
https://www.evernote.com

Here are a few suggestions for general storage and easy transfer between devices:

Google Drive (to set up your free google account if you do not have one)
https://www.google.com

Dropbox
https://www.dropbox.com

You should also consider "cloud" based backup for your computer files. There are many different plans to choose from. Here are a few suggestions.

Crashplan
http://www.crashplan.com

MozyHome
http://mozy.com/home

Backblaze
http://www.backblaze.com

Strategies for Time Management & Good Organization

How to Get Projects Done Faster

Time management is vital to the success of your business, especially as an entrepreneur. We all deal with things differently so there really isn't a "one size fits all" system offered in this book. Instead, I've decided to include time management strategies that work for the majority.

How To Choose The Best Solution For You

The best way to figure out which of the solutions will work best for you is to simply give each one a try. Be patient with yourself. You're going to be creating a lot of useful new habits. You will most likely find that combining more than one strategy will give you even better results.

The most important thing is to get started.

Choose Your Tools

To begin with, you're going to want to choose your method for planning and creating your to-do list.

There are so many great virtual tools these days and of course if you're someone who just loves to put pen to paper, a good old fashioned daily planner will be perfect for you.

It took me a long time to make the transition from using a physical planner and calendar to using something in a digital format. That's how much I love writing things down and for many, the simple act of physically crossing something off your list means a lot! I did finally make the change because I have a strong commitment to being location independent and this comes with having as little physical gear for my business as possible.

Here I will just tell you what I have used (after much research) and loved myself. You are sure to find plenty of other great apps and online tools by doing some simple searches yourself.

I've used Franklin Covey planners in the past and would highly recommend these systems for people who like to use pen and paper. There are many beautiful binders and planning sheets to choose from.

http://franklinplanner.fcorgp.com/store/

Currently I use 2 main apps on my smartphone for planning purposes.

For my calendar, I use Week Calendar which can sync with your Google calendars.
http://www.weekcal.com

For my main to-do lists, I use (and adore!) an app called 2Do.
http://www.2doapp.com

Make A Schedule

One of the trickier things about being in business for yourself, especially at the beginning, often has to do with keeping a schedule.

It is very easy to relish in your newfound freedom regarding the fact that you can now choose the hours and days that you wish to work. This can definitely be a big trap if you do not have clear intentions about your schedule and the amount of time that you want to devote to the success of your business.

Since you are reading this book about time management, I will assume that you could benefit from some good scheduling.

If nothings else, this can help you to start to develop some really good work habits. If you do not have the intention of working during certain times of day, it can be way too easy to procrastinate…watching TV, cleaning, chatting on the phone or whatever else would fill your normal non-working hours.

I suggest that you begin by getting very clear about the number of hours that you do want to put into your business each week. From here, determine the days of the week that you want to take off, if any at all. For some people, especially starting out, working every day along with some time off every day can yield the most benefits. On the other hand, you might really benefit from a day that is completely free of business tasks. Only you know what that best scenario will be for you.

Until you get this down, I would plan out your work schedule in terms of actual days and hours you will work, in your calendar. It is important that you really commit to your work time as it will be essential to ramp up your productivity.

In the next section, we'll talk about scheduling blocks of time.

Schedule Blocks Of Time

You can decide what hours you want to work during the day. This can largely depend on the type of person you are and whether you prefer mornings or are a night owl.

I am a very early morning person myself and find that I feel the best at 5:00AM, or in some cases even earlier, depending on how much sleep I've gotten. I really can NOT do creative work at night, so I need to adjust my schedule to do tasks that fit with how I am feeling at certain times each day.

I like to look at my schedule in terms of chunking project tasks during certain times of day.

As an example, since I am feeling the most creative (perhaps after my first cup of coffee) in the early morning, I might schedule a first writing session of the day for 6-8AM. In general, I'd get up around 5AM, have some coffee, check e-mail and social media platforms and get myself settled for a 6AM start. This doesn't mean that I would write non-stop for 2 hours. I'd take little breaks to get up out of my chair at least once every hour and I suggest that you do this too.

I would then plan for a work break - some news, breakfast and some exercise.

I would then schedule another block of time while still at my best energy level from around 10-1. During this time I would try to also get some more intense project work done as I know I'll be heading into a bit of an energy slump (my pattern) soon.

I tend to have lunch and then a bit of a rest/siesta right after.

My ideal afternoon would have another good chunk of time to cross things off my to-do list.

After dinner, I'm more likely to have something playing on TV (a guilty pleasure) and during this time I can work on more technical tasks or items that don't require a lot of mental energy or creativity from me.

This is just an example of how I structure many of my days. You will design a schedule that works the best for you and adjust accordingly.

The main point that I am making here is that it might be the most beneficial to plan in your rest/break periods (because they will happen anyways) and really utilize those work blocks of time to best suit your energy level and the particulars of your business.

If you run a service related business, your schedule might be more dependent on certain times. These are factors that you will have to take into account and perhaps manage the expectations of your clients when it comes to your hours of business.

Create Systems

I am such a believer in creating systems when it comes to running your business. Even if you are the only person currently working in your business, treat this suggestion as if you are about to hire employees.

Constantly be thinking about each set of tasks that you do within your business and how you can best systematize a process. Even if you don't plan on hiring someone for a very long time, if ever, this can really help with streamlining the things that you do on a regularly basis. Ultimately this will lead to better time management and higher levels of productivity.

Create a written manual of procedures for your business, writing out your systems of operation just as you would if you wanted it handed over to a new employee.

Here are some examples of procedures that you could systematize, using our self-published author role as the example.

*how to deal with fan email
*creating a Facebook campaign that is effective
*a procedure for daily interactions on Twitter
*the process of outlining a new novel
*the process of researching for a new novel
*book launch procedure
*procedure for doing a free book promotion

Basically anything that you do regularly can by broken down into a procedure. This will help you to gain clarity yourself and also put you in a very good position if and when you do decide to outsource some of your business tasks.

The Pareto Principle: Finding Your Critical 20%

The Pareto Principle also referred to as "Pareto's Law" or the "80/20 rule" gets its name from Vilfredo Pareto. He was an economist living in Italy in the early part of the 1900's. The 80/20 rule according Pareto concluded that about 20% of the people controlled about 80% of the land in Italy.

It was his way of showing the unfair and lopsided distribution of wealth.

So how does the Pareto Principle help you as an entrepreneur?

Today the 80/20 Rule can be applied quite well to time management. Several best sellers have been written about the 80/20 rule and there are Fortune 500 companies who swear by this theory.

The theory behind the 80/20 rule when it comes to time management is that you should make a point to focus on the 20% of your tasks, projects, products, etc…that will have the most impact on your business. Typically this 20% is what will increase your bottom line and move you forward.

When I was just getting started as an entrepreneur, I would often ask myself the following question when looking at my daily task list.

"What, on this list, is the fastest path to cash?"

This question can really help you to focus on the items that matter most to your business on a daily basis.

How to Use the Pareto Principle In Your Business

Focus the majority of your time, expertise and energy on the most important tasks (That's the 20%.) and you'll not only end up successfully completing your projects, you will also avoid wasting time working on meaningless items that don't offer great impact to your business.

For this example, we'll identify a typical task list for a self-published author.

Write or Revisit Your Goals for the Week

Take a sheet of paper (or look at the list you've already created during your goal setting session) and list your main projects and areas of focus for the week ahead. For a writer who is working on a new book, a good portion of the week will probably be devoted to writing.

Here is an example goal list for a week:
*write 10,000 words on new novel #2
*set up a free promotion for novel #1 (already published)
*research to find a new cover designer
*create new twitter background
*read for pleasure/research within chosen genre
*create an e-mail follow-up sequence
*create a plan for Facebook promotion that is more organized than current

Prioritize Your Day Making the Critical 20% the Priority

Now, let's assume that it is a Monday and we are creating our daily to-do list with the weekly goals in front of us.

In our example, besides the items listed for the week, let's say that you'd like to get your car cleaned, dye your hair (yourself) because it is driving you crazy, return a phone call to your old college friend and schedule a regular check-up appointment with your dentist.

Now you've got a lot of things to prioritize.

Many of us will find ourselves getting totally distracted by the non-business list and never actually get to those highly effective items on the list. In this case your 20% is firstly going to be everything that is focused on getting the novel #2 published. This means that focusing your first and best energy on getting that daily writing count in will ultimately be pushing you forward within your business.

Even the twitter background task and the e-mail follow-up items, should come after your writing session which is likely to create some good momentum for you at the start of your work day.

If you are just getting started with a service type business and acquiring clients is your main focus, your priorities and your 20% are going to be focused on the things you need to do to get those meetings which will lead to contracts and money in your pocket. Those items might be things like sending emails, making cold calls, conducting research to see who you can connect with and attending local networking events. Other business tasks not related to actually getting and servicing the client, will be within your 80%.

Focus on getting the critical tasks done and you'll find that the time it takes to complete important projects often diminishes. You will also find that the quality of your work goes up as well. That's because when you spend the majority of your time working on the parts of your business that are the most important, not only will you get it done faster, but you will have the time to pay closer attention to details.

How to Put Your To-Do List on Steroids!

Judging from the title of this section alone you might be thinking I'm going to suggest some cool software or app for your iPhone. Although there are a ton of productivity programs and apps out there (see my suggestions throughout the book), for now I'm going to ask you to keep it simple.

Keeping and maintaining a to-do list can help you keep up with client services, phone calls, marketing your business, new ideas and just about anything else you can think of to help make running your business from home successful.

Sometimes we can get caught up in the "shiny new object" syndrome. This is when a new product or tool comes out and convinces us that if we buy it suddenly everything will work perfectly. Well if that were true, there wouldn't be yet another new "thing" released literally every other week!

To get the most out of your to-do list, you're going to need a simple notebook that will only be used for writing down what needs to get done. It doesn't need to be anything fancy.

The purpose of going the "old school pen and paper route" has to do with the way we process information. When you write something down, read it and reread it over again, you are more likely to retain the information to memory. When you create a to-do list via some kind of software for example, it doesn't have the same effect on your brain. Have you ever added something to your Google calendar, set a reminder pop-up and then not really remembered even putting that information on the calendar in the first place?

Think about how you feel when you see an electronic reminder pop-up. Do you feel annoyed and either dismiss the reminder or snooze it for another 15 minutes? More than likely it doesn't bother you to turn it off all together but when you have a list of things to do that is written in your own handwriting there is a stronger mind body connection.

There's something really satisfying about taking your pen and drawing a line through a task you've completed. I find it a lot more motivating to move on to the next task just because I like the feeling I get when I cross off another accomplishment in my day!

That's why I believe the act of physically writing your to-do list makes it more likely you'll complete various tasks. We all like the good feelings associated with success. Each item on your list is a small success.

How To Create Your Business To-Do List

Take that simple notebook and divide one page into 4 sections. At the top of each section write the following:

Section 1 - "Things that must be done today" (Here insert a window of time e.g. 1PM- 4PM)
Section 2 - "Things I need to work on"(9AM - 10AM)
Section 3 - "Things I should work on each day" (4PM – 5 PM)
Section 4 - " Notes"

Don't overwhelm yourself with too many tasks. If you are managing your time accordingly, then you won't be overwhelmed. If you do find that you have too many things to do, you need to change the way you're spending your time so that you can spread your projects out throughout the week.

Next, go to each section and write down no more than 3 tasks for each.

Section 1 should be things that require the most time and effort to be completed. They could also be important phone calls or emails that have to be taken care of above all else. You are the only one who can determine what is a "section 1" task as it depends on the type of business you're in and what services or products you provide to clients and customers.

Section 2 tasks are things that you need to work on and will eventually end up as section 1 items on another day.

Section 3 tasks are things that you will need to work on the next day. These should be written at the end of your work day and may include daily tasks. For example, managing your email, marketing and social media management might be considered section 3 types of tasks. The tasks in section 3 should not require a lot of time, as they are tasks you do on a daily basis.

Finally, use the space in section 4 to make notes about any issues you may have had completing a task. This is going to be important later on. After about two weeks of using this system, you can take a look at your notes. Chances are you will begin to see a pattern of something you're doing that is keeping you from getting certain tasks done. Use this information to make adjustments and watch your productivity increase.

Using Sticky Notes - This Still Works!

If you're among the technology challenged, some of those old school methods of time management are still effective. When you really think about it, most of the apps and other software used to help entrepreneurs like yourself are just new and improved techie versions of old methods.

Sticky notes can help you keep track of projects, to do lists, phone calls, emails and just about anything else.

Color

You can find sticky notes in a wide range of colors. I suggest buying one of those multi colored packs. Office supply stores as well as neighborhood drugstores carry sticky notes.

How To Use Sticky Notes For Time Management

Divide your sticky notes into different stacks by color. Each color should be associated with the importance level of the task. So here's an example:

Red = High priority (May have specific due dates)

These are tasks that should be taken care of first.

Orange = Important

The tasks in this color category may be things that need to be done but may not yet be high priority. For example, it's a Monday morning and you need to have a proposal to a prospective new client on Thursday. You still have time to get it done. However, if you still haven't completed the task by Wednesday than you should move this task to the Red – High priority category.

Blue = Ongoing

These are tasks that you do on a regular basis. These might be things like networking, blogging, marketing, advertising etc.

Green = Completed Projects/Tasks

Major projects and other tasks that have been completed each week should be written on the green notes. You'll add to those items at the end of each work week.

Each task should have its own sticky note. You can attach your notes to your wall directly or purchase an inexpensive white board. Every time you complete one of your tasks, remove the appropriate note.

Why Using Sticky Notes Works So Well

When you use sticky notes, you have an instant visual representation of what needs to get done and when. As you complete each task and remove the note you will feel a sense of accomplishment. Placing completed tasks on a green note allows you to see how efficiently you've worked all week.

Sometimes we can get so caught up with trying to get things done that it can be quite motivating to see how much you actually got done during the week.

If, at the end of the week, you notice that there are still red and orange items that you haven't dealt with yet, this would be an indication that you're not managing your time well and adjustments need to be made.

The Benefits of Getting Up an Hour Earlier

How many times have you been faced with some kind of deadline and wished there were more hours in a day? We've all been there. One way to get more time out of a 24 hour day is to add one extra hour.

The way to do that is to simply get up an hour earlier than normal. Of course you're not creating an additional "25th hour" but you are creating an additional one hour to your day. We spend a certain number of hours each day sleeping, working, running errands, socializing, spending time with family, putting out fires and tons of other things that are all a part of daily life.

When you need more time to deal with an area of your life (like an entrepreneurial endeavor), the key to getting that extra time can simply be to get up an hour earlier each day.

So if, for instance, you need more time to work on marketing your business, use that hour to get the most essential tasks done first within that area.

How to Plan Your Extra Hour

Step 1

When you write your daily to-do list, be sure to include a special section on your list and give it a title. You can call it anything you want.

Here are a few ideas:

"My Extra Hour"
"My Power Hour"
"First Things First"

Step 2

Write down what you want to get done during that hour and make sure to only work on those tasks.

Ideally, you should only have one major project to focus on during that hour. It may take more than one hour to complete the specific project, but don't try to work on more than one major thing at a time. Otherwise you'll end up overwhelming yourself.

Step 3

In order for this technique to work, you have to be committed to giving all of your attention to that one project or area of your business. Don't stop to check e-mail if that is not a task needed to get what you're working on done.

Why This Method Works

When you give that hour a specific title like the ones in the example above, you are also giving it a higher level of importance. It's a mental cue to treat that time as special and it increases the likelihood that you will actually complete whatever it is you need to get done.

Plus when you set your alarm to wake up a full hour earlier than usual, you are also sending a message to yourself subconsciously that the project is really important and worth getting up an hour earlier to get it done.

You won't know just how effective this can be until you give it a try. So if you have something that needs more time and attention to detail, consider using this strategy to get it done.

How Limiting Some Conveniences Can Force You To Work More Efficiently

One day while working from home my Internet service stopped working right in the middle of a new book I was working on. After calling my service provider and after wasting time on hold "for the next available customer service agent" for several long minutes, I was really frustrated as I rely a lot on being able to go online to do research and other related tasks. So I gathered up all of my notes and my laptop and headed to my local library which had free WI-FI access and stayed open until 9PM.

I got there around 1:30PM or so and was about to begin working when I noticed a sign stating that they would be closing early due to some maintenance issue that had to be dealt with. Instead of closing at their usual 9PM time, they would be closing at 4PM!

I knew I needed the extra time to work and wasn't prepared to have my "work hours" cut short, but I had no other choice. So I sat down and got to work. I had a deadline to make and made the decision to get it done by 4PM.

The "Aha" Moment

A few hours later I had completed the project with time to spare. It was only 3:30 PM! I was really surprised that I had not only finished what I needed to do but had also gotten it done before the 4PM closing time. Then I noticed something I hadn't when I first arrived. I took another look at the sign and realized that the date was for the previous day! They hadn't gotten around to taking the signs down!

That meant I still had until 9PM to work, but I was already finished. That's when I started to realize something. When I thought I had a very limited window to get something done I was totally focused on getting the work completed. This was a lot different from giving myself a time limit under circumstances where I had control. In other words, if I had been at home with the Internet working, I would have given myself a lot more leeway to get something done because I didn't have to rush. Having to work under the belief that I only had access to the Internet for a few hours versus several hours, forced me to focus on getting the work done a lot quicker.

Not having the convenience of being able to "slack off", made me work a lot more efficiently. I didn't have time to waste, so I had to get it done.

I'm not suggesting that you cancel your Internet service or anything else you use to run your business. What I am suggesting is taking at least one day a week and going to work in an environment that you do not control. You'll also need to make sure you cannot sit there for more than an hour or two.

For example, many coffee shops, restaurants and cafes have free WiFi. Look for the smaller mom and pop kind of businesses that aren't likely to allow you to just sit there all day using their WiFi without spending money there first.

Choose something that usually takes you longer than 45 minutes to an hour to complete. Not because that's how long it takes, but because you'd typically be stopping to do something else or you'd get distracted by phone calls, e-mails or whatever. Make sure it's something that has to be done that day by a certain time.

Then challenge yourself to go somewhere like one of the places mentioned above where you may only have an hour to get your work done. You'll be amazed at how much you can get done when you're "on the clock" so to speak. The normal distractions won't even bother you because you will be in a higher state of "get it done" mode.

This isn't something you have to do all the time but whenever you feel like you're not giving it your all, this can be a good way to boost your productivity and give yourself a mental jolt!

Technology Short Cuts to Help You Get Things Done

In this section, I want to focus specifically on using technology to manage your time. There are a lot of great programs and apps out there to take a look at and you are sure to find something that will suit your needs.

Timers

Simple timers can be used to keep you aware of how much time you're spending on any one task. You can opt to use an old fashioned kitchen timer, stopwatch, timer apps for your smartphone or simple digital countdown timers on your PC or Mac.

Personally I find timers that make loud ticking sounds a bit distracting. I get so paranoid listening to the time go by that I can barely focus on what I'm trying to do! Digital countdown timers work very well and are quiet until the time is up.

Once you decide which timer you want to use, you're going to set a specific amount of time to get whatever it is you're working on completed. The easiest way is to simply jot down how much time you want to allot to each task and reset your timer to that time when you begin to work on a new task.

A simple Google search online will find several options if you want some type of virtual timer for your computer or smartphone.

By default, the iPhone has a nifty countdown timer built into the clock settings. You can also search for additional iPhone or Android apps that you can use for this purpose.

Q10

There is a free program called Q10. If your business requires you to write reports, proposals, sales material, copy writing etc...this neat little program eliminates all "on screen" distractions. All those icons on your desk top, browsers, games and everything else disappears when you launch Q10. Don't worry because nothing gets deleted or moved around on your computer.

When you launch Q10, your PC becomes totally black. Once you begin to type, the only thing you will see are the words that you are typing from your computer's keyboard. There are no distractions from icons or anything else on your PC's desktop. It even has the sound of an old fashioned electric typewriter as you type and the old school sound of an electric carriage return! Pretty cool!

It's amazing how much time this can save you. The level of focus you will experience is nothing short of amazing. You can get your normal screen back by hitting the Ctrl-Q on your computer. This only works on PC's and is very simple to use. It doesn't come with a lot of information as far as use because it is so simple. Just remember to press F1 on your keyboard and a nice little box will pop up with a list of all of the commands you can use.

Q10 has a built in timer you can set to keep yourself focused on whatever you're working on. It also has a built in auto correct feature, spell checker and it can keep track of your progress for you as well.

http://www.baara.com/q10/

BookedIn

BookedIn is a free to very low cost service that allows you to book appointments via your website. Once you open an account you simply fill out some basic information about your business. This includes things like your name, address, phone number, business hours and availability. You'll be given easy instructions on how to embed your BookedIn calendar on your website.

If, for instance, you offer free or paid consultations for your services, new clients can book time based on the times and days you specify in BookedIn. If you charge for consultations, clients or customers can pay via PayPal before they can book an appointment.

Imagine how much time you'll save! You'll receive an email when someone books time with you, so you can prepare accordingly. There is no phone or e-mail tag to take up valuable time.

http://getbookedin.com

Hello Fax/Hello Sign

The more efficiently you can manage your business, the better time management becomes. Online services like Hello Fax/Hello Sign can help you do just that. Instead of spending money on fax machines, toner, paper and eventual repairs, you can have a virtual fax number instead. All of your faxes are sent to you via email. You can also send faxes right from your PC. You can create fax cover sheets as a template too.

Hello Sign is another service by the same company. If your business requires clients to sign contracts, you can send them via email. Electronic signatures are accepted under the US. Federal ESIGN Act. I'm not a lawyer so it's a good idea to check with an attorney who concentrates in contract law to be on the safe side.

Both services offer free and paid versions and both will save you a lot of time overall.

https://www.hellofax.com
https://www.hellosign.com

Virtual Phone numbers

To make sure you control how you're contacted, it's always a good idea to have a separate business number. For some work from home entrepreneurs, it can get a bit expensive. Virtual phone numbers allow you to have a local or toll-free number which you can forward to any phone you want. You can also set up voice mail and schedule all calls to automatically go to your virtual number after hours.

There are several companies out there to choose from, but not all offer the same services. So before you sign up, make sure the one you choose has the features you need. Some virtual phone number companies like Evoice for example, even have phone apps that allow you to call from your personal cell phone. Instead of your cell number showing up on a client's caller ID, your virtual number would show, allowing you to keep your personal number private.

FreedomVoice
http://www.freedomvoice.com

Evoice
http://www.evoice.com

HostedNumbers
http://www.hostednumbers.com

Time Management Apps

There are thousands of productivity apps available for smartphones. Choosing the best one depends on what your own personal needs and preferences might be.

Tips For Choosing The Right App For You

1. Check the features of each app to be sure it has all of the capabilities you're looking for.

2. See how many times an app has been downloaded and then read the reviews. Beware of apps with 5 star ratings and only one or two reviews. Typically these are reviews left by the developer in an attempt to get more people to download their app. Apps with hundreds or thousands of reviews is a much better way to get an idea of how well an app performs.

3. Make sure you read the fine print. Many free apps come with advertising that can be obtrusive and very annoying. Free typically in the app world can come at a price. This could be ads, promotional pop-ups and even privacy issues.

4. Take advantage of free trials. This is a great way to take productivity apps for a test drive before shelling out cash. Make sure it does what it advertises. Use it as you plan to when you purchase it to make sure it's easy to use.

5. Stick with well known app makers whenever possible or those with good track records. Unfortunately, anyone on the planet can make an app and put it up for sale online. In my opinion you have a better chance at getting a high quality app for iPhones than Android. That's because the quality control is a lot higher with Apple. Google allows anyone to submit to the Android marketplace with very little control in terms of quality. That's not to say you can't find quality apps for Android. Just be aware and do your research first.

Apps for smartphones are still in the "wild wild west" mode so you may end up trying out several before you find one that meets your criteria. Another idea is to ask business associates, family and friends if they can recommend a solid time management app.

Time Tracking Apps:

Eternity Time Log
http://www.komorian.com/eternity.html

OfficeTime
http://www.officetime.net

To-Do List Apps:

2Do
http://www.2doapp.com

Wunderlist
https://www.wunderlist.com

Save Time Using Software to Help You Keep Track of Clients

CRM

Zoho.com is a complete CRM or Client Relationship Management system that is based online. You can set up an account and keep track of e-mail correspondence, manage client projects, create documents and even collaborate and make changes as you work on various projects with clients. You can get started for free. There are some components that remain free and others will require a monthly fee if you choose to use those services.

The advantage of using online based CRM systems is convenience. You can access your client information from any PC with an Internet connection.

http://www.zoho.com

Yesware E-mail

If you rely on e-mail a lot to run and acquire new business, Yesware is an easy to use free client tracking software. Basically, you are able to track who views your e-mails and manage the prospecting process as well. To use Yesware you must have a Gmail address. Once you sign up, Yesware will automatically install in the Gmail account of your choice. As of this writing, you can track and send up to 100 emails free per month. If you require more there is a monthly fee.

The advantage of being able to track your prospecting email activity can save you time by giving potential clients a higher priority and following up with them faster.

http://www.yesware.com

Free Office Software

If you're on a budget consider using Google for creating documents, spreadsheets, slide show presentations, calendars and even video conferencing. You must have a Gmail account to access all of the above.

Once you set up your free Google account, you will automatically have access to free cloud hard drive space to store all of your documents. It's called Google Drive. You can then create folders for each client or different areas of your business that you need to keep organized. You can even share documents securely with clients.

Sign up for Google Plus and you can use Google Hang Outs for live video conferencing with clients.

The biggest advantage to using Google products is the ease of use and the fact that the services are free.

The disadvantages have to do with control. Google can decide to discontinue a product or service at anytime. Although they will give you advance notice, it's still something to keep in mind. Also Google is not known for customer service. So if something fails you're pretty much on your own.

You can create a free account and get started with everything Google related here.

http://www.google.com

Open Office

OpenOffice is an office suite similar to Microsoft Office. Everything you can do with MS Office you can also do with Open Office. This software is completely free and was created by Oracle and is now owned and managed by Apache. Both companies are known worldwide and are leaders in their industry. You can open, create and save documents in several different formats including all MS Word extensions.

http://www.openoffice.org

Outsourcing to Leverage Your Time

Sooner or later your business will grow to the point where you're going to need additional help. If you don't have the budget to take on a full time employee, outsourcing can be a tremendous asset when it comes to time management.

Delegating tasks to someone else allows you to spend more time working on the key areas of your business that will help you grow and become more profitable.

How to Get Started

Before you run out looking for someone, you have to sit down and write out exactly what you want an individual to do for you. Trust me, if you don't know the specifics beforehand you are going to waste a lot of time and money.

Get The Details Right First

1. Make a list of the specific duties you want to delegate. It's not enough to just say you want someone to respond to e-mails. If you want someone to respond to support e-mails, for example, then the person you hire needs to have specialized knowledge.

2. Will the person you hire need special skills? If so, what? Things like the ability to read and write fluently in the language of your choice is a top priority. Will they need graphic skills? Accounting background? If they will be engaging in some form of lead generation, do they have a solid background in sales and telemarketing?

3. Ask yourself some questions also. How much can you afford to spend? Are you okay with hiring someone who may be based in another country?

4. You'll also have to train the person that you hire. That might entail creating a SOP manual (Standard Operating Procedures) to make sure that they follow specific steps.

Yes, it can be time consuming to find, hire and eventually outsource various parts of your business. So you want to do so only when you have the time and patience to find the right person and make sure that they are trained properly.

You may be tempted to take short cuts just to hurry up get some extra help, but if you do, you'll run the risk of getting someone who isn't qualified to do the work at an acceptable level. Remember, the person you choose will be representing your business. So make sure you make the effort to find the right individual for the job.

There are a lot of other steps to outsourcing which go way beyond the scope of this book. I would suggest doing a Google search for outsourcing companies as a start.

Here are some of the most popular websites to find individuals available for outsourcing.

http://fiverr.com

https://www.elance.com

https://www.odesk.com

http://www.guru.com

Jedi Mind Trick To Automatically Put You In "Get it Done Now" Mode

This "mind trick" probably won't stop storm troopers from invading your home office, but it will force you to make a decision between getting something done or wasting more time.

Ready?

The next time you find yourself in a position where something should be taken care of now rather than later, here's what I want you to do.

Stop. Take a deep breath and say this out loud:

"Is the choice I'm about to make going to bring me closer to my goal or push me further away?"

Automatically you're going to start mentally questioning yourself and your choice. You will begin to think a little harder about not doing whatever it is that should be taken care of at the time. It forces you to take a look at what you're doing in the moment. When you ask yourself this question your mind starts to think about the longer term ramifications of not doing a specific task and keeping commitments to yourself.

Now, I'm not going to tell you that you're going to opt to go ahead and get whatever it is done every single time. We're all human and we all make poor choices from time to time, but the more you become increasingly conscious of your day to day decisions, the more you will choose the task over other things that just distract from your business goals.

Why?

It's a psychological thing. It's like a little nagging voice inside that almost forces you to be accountable and take care of business or suffer the consequences. In business, the consequences of lost time and money can be great motivators.

Write that sentence down and post it in your home office space where you can see it. The next time you want to do something you know wouldn't be the best choice, read it out loud and see what happens.

Keeping A Calendar To Stay Organized

Using a simple calendar to keep track of daily tasks is another tool to help you manage your time better.

A desk or wall calendar can be great for allowing you to quickly see what's scheduled at a glance while you are working. Consider using colored markers for different categories. Just as I suggested with sticky notes, colors stand out and can bring different things to your attention faster.

Even if you're using a to-do list, a calendar is another way to track and enforce the importance of getting things done. You can make a calendar that is your main system or use it as a back-up. It really depends on what works best for you.

A friend of mine uses the sticky note method I went over in the previous section. She also has a big wall calendar with basically the same information. When she's on a call with a client, she glances at the wall calendar when discussing specific dates and time frames. For her, it works better than rifling through the pages of her to-do lists.

A calendar is also great if you have to make in person visits with clients. Many people prefer a date book with plenty of space for notes that can be carried and used while on the go. You can also use the calendar function on your smartphone if you have one. Although sometimes adding notes from a meeting and inputting it into a smartphone isn't always as easy or practical as simply writing it down. You can always add key notes to your phone later.

There are many different calendar and planner type tools that can suit a wide variety of needs, so it shouldn't be a problem finding something that will work for you and your business.

The Multitasking Myth

The term multitasking has become the go to word for a lot of employers in an attempt to get employees to get more work done. Employers like to throw that word around when they want you to do the job of two or three individuals, because it saves them money not having to pay additional salaries. Or maybe they want something else done in addition to what you already have on your plate, so they tell you to multitask and you'll get it all done!

Tah dah!!!

So it's no wonder that when you begin working from home, it's easy to fall into the trap of thinking you can multitask your way to success. Instead, what ends up happening is that you get overwhelmed with way too much to get done in a short period of time all because you believe you can multitask everything.

Multitasking Isn't What You Think It Is

Let me explain. Multitasking for most people is the ability to do more than one thing at a time. That might mean working on more than one project simultaneously, while still being able to run meetings, errands and a long list other things. The belief is that if you can do a lot of different tasks at the same time, you're multitasking.

The Problem

The problem is that our brains do not have the ability to give 100% of our focus to more than one thing at a time. So, if you are splitting your attention in order to get several things done, I can almost guarantee that you're going to end up making some major mistakes somewhere that may not have been made if you were instead giving your undivided attention to one task at a time. It doesn't matter what it is you're trying to do, the results will be the same.

Here's an example:

In almost every state in the US it is now illegal to drive a car and talk on your cell phone unless you're wearing a headset. The reason is to keep drivers from being distracted on the road. When you're trying to talk to someone and also trying to pay attention while you drive, your brain has to choose which one to give its undivided attention to. Think about it. Have you ever been on your cell phone talking while you were driving and missed an exit that you take every day? Or ran a stop sign or almost had an accident because you didn't realize the car ahead of you had stopped?

I saw a video on the news where a guy was so focused while texting on his phone that he walked off the subway platform! Lucky for him that another person pulled him to safety as a train was just seconds away.

The reason dangerous things like in the above examples happen, is because the brain is trying to "multitask" and do more than one thing at a time but it cannot. We're not wired that way. Recently, researchers announced that wearing a headset while driving doesn't reduce the likelihood of getting into an accident.

Duh!

That's why I say that multitasking by the most common definition is a myth. That's not to say you can't work on more than one thing at a time. You can. Just don't expect your best work to be the end result. You end up getting mentally fatigued and that's when mistakes happen.

So Now What?

My best advice is to plan your work using one or more of the methods I've given you in this book. Planning out time schedules and creating workable plans within a reasonable amount of time is the best way to go.

Try not to take on projects at the last minute or if you have a full schedule already. The lure of making money often makes many entrepreneurs take on too much fearing times when work may be slow.

To keep that from happening, make sure you are always marketing your business. If you have a constant stream of inquiries about your business you won't have to worry about the "feast or famine" syndrome that so many work from home entrepreneurs deal with.

The Best Time of Day To Get The Most Difficult Tasks Done

One of my favorite shows to watch was Fear Factor. You know the show where you could win $50K after doing a series of scary stunts and also usually eating something really gross? Whenever there was a challenge to eat more than one disgusting thing, I noticed many contestants would opt to eat the worse thing first, just to get it out of the way.

Author Brian Tracy wrote a book that is now considered a classic called Eat That Frog. If that makes you squeamish, that's great! It's supposed to, unless of course, you actually like eating frogs! In any case, the point of that book is in my opinion one of the best strategies for getting difficult tasks done. It's the same strategy those contestants used on Fear Factor.

Do the most difficult task first (eat that frog) and the rest of your day is literally a piece of cake! Whatever it is that you most dread doing for the day should go at the very top of your to-do list before everything else. Perhaps it will be your early morning "power hour" item. Then you must actually do the thing on your list!

Why Do The Tough Items First?

How you start your day tends to set the stage for the rest of your day. Raise your hand if you've ever gone to work after not sleeping well and spent the entire day in a bad mood? The same thing can happen if you choose to do the easiest items on your list first. If you start your day doing all of the easy things, you're not going to be too happy knowing in the back of your mind that you still have to deal with that difficult task, project, phone call or whatever it may be. Instead, if you get up and focus on getting that difficult task done, you can go about the rest of your day feeling pretty good about yourself.

It's done and out of the way!

Besides, the later you wait to start on a difficult task the greater the risk of you not doing it at all or not doing the best job you could.

Getting It Done!

Step 1

Take a look at your to-do list and choose one item that you're dreading. It's the one that makes you roll your eyes towards the ceiling every time you think about it!

Step 2

Move it to the top of your list and plan to tackle it as the first thing you do when you start your day. In a previous section, I talked about the benefits of getting up an hour earlier each day. If you haven't read that section please do so as that hour may be the best time for you to eat that frog!

Step 3

Stay consistent and notice how much time you are able to save. Plus when you get the tough stuff out of the way earlier, you're less likely to spend your personal time trying to catch up.

Create A 30 Day Challenge

I am a big believer in making strong commitments to yourself in order to create some massive momentum.

I like to do 30 day challenges whenever I want to experiment or create a new habit for myself. The key is to think of something that over 30 days could really create a positive change within your life. In the context of this book, we are focusing on business productivity.

Think of one thing that you could commit to doing for 30 days without fail and vow to give this your best shot, if nothing else, for the experiment of it all.

Here are some examples,

If you are a writer having a difficult time with the actual "writing" part of your business, (Hey, we've all been there.) perhaps you could challenge yourself to get up 1 hour earlier than normal JUST to dedicate to your writing first thing of the day. If mornings are not a good time for you, choose another challenge that involves making this one hour of writing top priority. Imagine how it would feel at the end of a month having an additional 30 hours of writing to add to your current project?

If you are in a service related business that depends on acquiring new clients, maybe your challenge would be to send x number of e-mails per day and/or make x number of cold calls per day.

Assuming you have an online presence for your business (and you should!), your 30 day challenge might include 30 minutes of promotional activities each day. This could further be identified as social media management or whatever platform you feel would give the greatest impact to your business during this time.

Based on the types of tasks that you feel you "should" be doing for your business, you should have no trouble figuring out which types of things would be the best for you to target within a specific period of time.

Remind yourself of your vision and goals for YOUR business! And good luck!

Tips for Avoiding Time Traps & Overcoming Procrastination

Common Time Traps & How to Avoid Them

If you lined up 100 work from home entrepreneurs and asked them what are some of the biggest issues they face when it comes to managing their time, there's no doubt in my mind that the following issues would all rank pretty high.

There are probably at least 2 or 3 issues you may be having a hard time trying to deal with right now. I will give you a simple strategy to deal with each one and before you know it you'll be sailing through your work day and getting a lot more done with fewer interruptions.

Establish Your Work Hours

Hold yourself accountable for your business by setting real working hours. When you do that you are making it clear to yourself, your family and your clients that you are serious about your business.

Also, having specific working hours will help you to stay focused and get into work mode during that time. This is not to say that you can't be flexible with your time, because, after all, that's one of the reasons you decided to work for yourself.

Right?

But if you're not careful you'll end up not being a master of your time. Instead, you'll end up constantly trying to keep up with various aspects of your business yet never really accomplishing a whole lot. When you work for an employer you're always watching the clock to make sure you reach deadlines, make important phone calls and answer emails before quitting time. You should do the same for your own business.

Do yourself a favor and decide what your regular business hours will be and stick to it. If you're not a morning person, then start your business hours late morning. You can always give clients or customers a "window of time" when they can expect a response to phone calls and emails. You don't have to tell them you don't get up until 10:00AM! Keep that secret to yourself.

Choosing Working Hours

This can be a bit tricky because everyone has a different situation. If you have children who are in school, for example, you may have to adjust your hours around their schedule. In some cases, you may have to start your working hours much earlier in the day. Of course, the kind of business you're in also plays a part in what your hours will be.

Just make sure that you choose a span of time that makes sense for both your business and you. You may have to experiment in the beginning to find something that works best.

Time Is Money!

There's no right or wrong set of hours, but you need to decide when your work day begins and stick to it. Work from home entrepreneurs get so wrapped up in the freedom thing that they end up getting overwhelmed because they haven't established working hours. Working for someone else means you're expected to arrive at work by a certain time every work day. There are several reasons why this is so, but mainly it's so that an employer can track your work time and make sure they are getting a good ROI or return on investment in terms of what they pay you.

You should be doing the same. Keeping track of your time allows you to price your services and bill clients accordingly if you are in a service related business. You also need to be able to have a set amount of work time for various client projects to make sure that you're not working overtime on low paying projects.

If you are a writer, as another example, it is a good idea to track how long your writing projects take you so that you can get an idea of your return on investment for these types of hours also.

If you're willing to do that for someone else, then it should be something you're willing to do for the success of your own business. So make your time count and maintain consistent working hours.

How to Quit Working

It's so important to have an "end of the work day" routine. If you don't, you'll find yourself working more than you're sleeping. The reason this is so important when it comes to time management is simply because if you're over working yourself you may end up getting a lot less sleep. Lack of sleep means that at some point your body will not be operating at optimum levels. Eventually you'll end up catching up on your sleep during what should be working hours. This then can lead to missed deadlines, angry clients and ultimately loss of business and profits.

So it's crucial to create a regular routine that signals to you on a subconscious level that it's time to stop working and rest. You need to be able to refresh your body, your mind and your spirit so that you'll be ready to work the next business day.

Just as you've established the business hours for your business, you need to establish a routine of ending your work day. There are tons of ways to do this and here are a few ideas to get you started in the right direction.

Step 1

About a half an hour before the end of your work day begin cleaning up your work area and preparing for the following day. Make sure you have your to-do list for the next day prepared. If there is something you did not complete, don't work on it if at all possible after working hours. Add it as a priority on your to-do list for the next day.

Step 2

Do not take work to bed with you. Make your bedroom a "no work zone" no matter how tempting it may be. Besides, if you're married or have a significant other, they might not appreciate it if you're always working. Your friends and family deserve some free time with you too. Let after hour business calls go to voice mail and resist checking your e-mail after work hours.

You also need some personal time to unwind and pamper yourself. Thinking about work can interfere with your ability to get a good night of sleep so leave work in your office until the next morning.

Step 3

Make it a habit to lock up your home office just as you would if you were working for someone else. Chances are you wouldn't go back to work at midnight to work on a client file right?

So why do so at home just because you can?

Remember, one of the reasons you've chosen to become a work from home entrepreneur is to enjoy the freedoms that comes along with that choice. So take time to enjoy that freedom.

Make Sure Everyone Else is Aware Of Your Working Hours

It's funny. When you decide to work from home, your family, friends and even clients think "you're not really working" because you're at home! Maybe it's a psychological thing with people. I don't know why it is that people have this perception, but I can't stress how important it is to let the world know that just because you work from home, it doesn't mean you're available to them whenever they want.

How to Enforce Contact Rules With Family & Friends

Keep in mind that you have to control your time when you work from home. If family and friends keep dropping by unannounced or calling just to shoot the breeze, nip it in the bud right from the start.

One way to do this is to explain what your business is about and what is required to be successful. Then let them know that unless there is an emergency you will not be available during your business hours.

Here's an example of what you might say to a friend or family member.

"I work from home as a virtual assistant which means my clients pay me to manage a lot of important details. So in order to make sure I am providing quality service, I have to maintain consistent business hours. I would love to chat with you and hang out but only when I'm not working. My business hours are from 8AM to 4PM Monday through Friday. So unless it's an emergency please call or stop by after 4PM."

I know what you're thinking. "Yeah right...how am I going to enforce those rules?"

It's actually a lot easier than you realize.

Here's how to do it.

Once you've had a conversation like the example above, you can enforce your rules by making sure that you don't break the rules. That means not giving in and sticking to the hours you've established. Here's an example on how to deal with friends and family.

Scenario – A family member or friend calls you during business hours because she's bored and wants to chit-chat.

First, always be polite. Most of the people in your life aren't out to sabotage you. If they do not work from home, they have no idea how difficult time management can be. So in this scenario, ask if this is an emergency. If not, kindly remind your friend that you're working but you'll be happy to talk to her after 4PM or whatever time you've set as the end of your work day.

End the call as quickly as possible. Now, be prepared because there are some people who simply won't "get it" and you will have to take the same steps a few more times. It's really important that you remain consistent. If you give in you're sending mixed messages. Eventually, family and friends will get the message and stop contacting you during your business hours.

How to Stop Clients From Contacting You After Hours

I think somewhere in the universe there is a rule that says it's okay to call someone any old time because they work from home! In my experience, most clients respect my working hours and make an extra effort to not contact me until the following business day. Unfortunately, this isn't always the case and if you haven't experienced this phenomenon yet… give it time!

Here's the thing…if this is a problem for you now, I'm sorry to break it to you but it's your fault!

What?

Yep.

Just as you should set firm contact rules with your friends and family, you have to do the same with clients. Otherwise you are literally "teaching" them that's it's okay to contact you at any time. You have to let clients know what your contact policy is right from the beginning. This way you will avoid phone calls at 9PM to ask you questions about a project you're working on for them. Or my personal favorite, dropping by on the weekend because they knew you would be home and just wanted to go over some stuff regarding their project or your services. Argh!

Simple Step by Step Plan To Stop Clients From Contacting You After Hours

Step 1

Create a simple SOP (Standard Operating Procedures) manual for new clients. There are several things to include in this and much depends on the nature of your business, but for the purposes of this book on time management, I'll stick with the issues regarding client contact.

Step 2

List your hours of operation unless there is a mutually agreed upon change due to some unforeseen circumstance or emergency. Then list what is considered an emergency.

Include how you wish to be contacted. If by phone, include a contact number and hours. This is really important so that you don't tie up your time talking to clients on the phone unnecessarily. If you're a consultant for example, you may want to set up a system to allow your clients to book appointments on a weekly or monthly basis.

There's a great free booking system for this called BookedIn and you can check that out here:

http://getbookedin.com

You should also include how e-mail correspondence should take place. E-mails going back and forth can be very time consuming. If, however, you don't mind communicating this way, then you may want to stress that the best way to get in touch is via e-mail. State how long it may take to respond so that they're not sitting in front of their PC or staring at their smartphone waiting to hear back from you.

Trust me, this happens more often than you think! So it may be a good idea if it makes sense for your type of business to give an average response time or a simple "I will get back to you as quickly as possible" could be used as well.

If you value your time, don't give clients your personal home or cell numbers. Get a separate phone number for business only. If you're on a tight budget, there are several services available that will allow you to get a virtual local or 800 number for a very small monthly fee. Here are a few that you can check out:

FreedomVoice
http://www.freedomvoice.com

Evoice
http://www.evoice.com

HostedNumbers
http://www.hostednumbers.com

Have your client sign the SOP and make sure you give them a copy. Now in a perfect world every client would read the SOP and abide by it. For the most part, most will respect your time with no problem. But for those who insist on contacting you outside of business hours here's how to handle them.

Scenario- Client keeps calling you even though they know your contact rules.

The first time this happens, gently remind your client about your working hours and suggest that they take a look at the SOP manual for specific details. If your client continues to ignore your hours have a talk with him or her.

Example:

"Your time is valuable and so is mine, so in order to make sure I'm providing you with the best service as well as the best service to my other clients it's important that I maintain consistency when it comes to time. If you need to speak to me about something regarding your account, that's fine. Please call and make an appointment to do so. This way I can give you my undivided attention."

If a client calls after business hours, don't take the call. If they email you outside of whatever rules you've set up, then do not respond. If the client gets upset, calmly remind them what your hours are and that you will gladly get back to them during normal business hours.

This may feel uncomfortable at first, but this really is a normal business expectation. When you have a personal problem with a billing issue, as an example, and you call to complain but instead get a recording that says "Our customer service hours are 9AM to 5PM," you understand that your choice is to either leave a message or call back during business hours. The credit card company doesn't have some guy sitting by the phone just in case someone calls after business hours. You should take the same approach when it comes to your business.

Don't give in. If you give in even one time, you'll have a difficult time getting clients to play by your rules.

How to Manage Distractions Like Facebook & E-mail

It is so easy to lose track of time when you're reading that funny post on your Facebook wall or checking your e-mail for the 10th time in an hour! Phone calls can also eat up your time pretty quickly as well.

You can still engage in all three, but you have to do so with a virtual time clock ticking in your head. We have a built in "I think I'm wasting time" meter. It's just that often we choose to ignore it because whatever we're doing is a lot more fun than working.

Social Network Management

I'm picking on Facebook because most people who are active on Facebook spend a huge amount of time checking messages, chatting with friends, playing games and so on and so on. But the rules would be the same for any social networking site.

If you're on Facebook, Twitter, Foursquare, YouTube and a long list of other sites checking in a lot on your personal account during business hours, you're wasting time. Period. If whatever you're doing isn't focused on business you're also potentially missing out on making money for your business. Have fun on Facebook before or after your business hours.

If you think Facebook time is harmless try this exercise.

The next time you're on Facebook set a timer in another room and go back to your PC. The reason I suggest placing the timer in another room is because it can distract you. I want you to do whatever you normally do on Facebook in the same relaxed manner you're used to doing so. The idea is to get a realistic sample of how much time you spend hanging out on various sites that have nothing to do with work.

Do this every day for a week. Every time you log into Facebook or some other non work-related social networking site, start that timer. When you log out write down the number of minutes you spent on Facebook or other sites. At the end of the week add up all of those minutes.

Then write down on a piece of paper the following sentence:

"This week I spent (insert total number of minutes here during business hours) on Facebook (or other site) writing on my friends walls, looking at photos, videos, timelines etc...instead of doing (insert work related items here)."

Then write down what you could have gotten accomplished in that same amount of time when it comes to your business. Remember, you're only recording the time spent on Facebook during your established working hours. When you force yourself to see things in a tangible way, the impact is a lot stronger and will compel you to pay closer attention to how you're managing your time.

The only other exception to the Facebook rule is if you have a business page that requires you to manage and update frequently. However, even in this instance you should allot a specific amount of time for managing your business page. See the earlier section on strategies for time management for a simple way to create a daily business calendar to help you manage key areas of your business so that you don't waste time.

E-mail

I am guilty of getting sucked into checking e-mail constantly. Although the techniques I'm about to share with you have significantly reduced my addiction to checking my e-mail all the time, I admit it can still be a struggle.

For every business, but especially entrepreneurs working from home, e-mail is almost as important as having a mobile phone. Many times clients and potential new clients contact you almost entirely by e-mail. So there's no way you can avoid not checking your inbox. When you're first starting out, you will find yourself checking e-mail dozens of times a day. You might be waiting for that first e-mail from a new client you're prospecting or an order for your product or service.

If this sounds familiar, you have to focus your time on more important areas of your business. Instead of checking your e-mail and hoping you get that order, focus your time on marketing and networking for business instead.

Create Your Own E-mail SOP

I talked about creating a Standard Operating Procedure for clients and you should create one for yourself as well. In terms of e-mail, create a routine of checking your e-mail at specific times throughout your work day.

Here's an example:

As the first thing at the start of your work day, give yourself a specific amount of time to read and send e-mails. So for instance, you may decide that 30 minutes is enough time. If you have to send a client proposal by e-mail, make sure you've scheduled time to complete the proposal before you sit down to send the e-mail. This way all you have to do is write a quick note, attach the proposal and hit send.

Done!

Then schedule additional times to check e-mail. Maybe right after lunch and again about an hour before you end your work day.

Also make sure you're checking only work related e-mail. This way you will be more likely to stay focused on getting more done than sending an e-mail to your BFF about that cute cat video that went viral! Check personal e-mail during your break time or after work hours.

Avoiding 3 of The Most Common Time Traps

Working from home is something I wouldn't trade for the world! The key to doing so successfully depends a lot on being able to avoid some sneaky common time traps.

Trap #1 – Fun!

Yes you read that correctly. Having fun doing whatever you feel like when you should be working is one of the most difficult things to deal with. Imagine a warm sunny day outside your window and trying to ignore thoughts of going to the beach or the park to goof off for awhile. You wouldn't dream of doing that when you work for someone, or maybe you would but you wouldn't risk losing your job to do so.

When you work from home and have no one to hold you accountable it's a lot easier to convince yourself it's okay to skip work and go have some fun.

A good way to deal with the temptation of fun is to schedule some "fun time" during the week. Pick a time when your schedule permits without sacrificing work-related tasks. In fact, doing it this way can be a great incentive to get projects done earlier than promised. If you can discipline yourself to stay the course the rest of the time, your fun time getaway will be that much sweeter.

Trap # 2 – Television

If you're a reality show junkie or you just like watching television, this activity is a huge time killer. It's so easy to get totally engrossed in an episode of your favorite television program only to then realize that you've spent 2 hours doing nothing but watching TV. It really doesn't matter if it's a soap opera, a crime show or PBS. It's still time wasted.

To combat the urge to watch television, make sure you do not have one in your home office or within close proximity. If your spouse, kids or roommates have televisions ask them to either turn the sound down or watch with headphones. This way you won't be distracted by listening to that fantastic car chase scene!

Trap # 3 – Diet

I cover the subject of your diet and the affects it can have on your ability to focus and think more clearly in a lot more detail in the next section of the book, but I think it's important to touch on it a bit here as well.

Eating calories high in bad carbohydrates like white breads, sugar and flour will not only put weight on you but can also make you sluggish and sleepy. You may also experience "brain fog" where no matter how hard you try, you can't concentrate and get things done in a timely manner.

You can't tell your client that the reason their project isn't complete is because your diet sucks!

Make sure you make it a habit to eat healthier, not just during your business hours, but throughout your entire day. It will make a huge difference in the level of productivity and in your ability to solve problems more effectively.

How To Manage The Amount of Time Spent on Phone Calls

If you're in a service related business, the phone is going to ring and that's a good thing. You just have to have a system in place for managing phone calls in a way that is the most productive for you. Phone conversations can get long and before you know it, you're behind on something you were working on and will have to spend personal time trying to get it done.

Here's how to manage your time when taking business calls.

Clients

Check the caller ID when a call comes in. If it's from a current client and you're expecting their call because they've followed your procedures and made an appointment, you should be prepared in advance.

Jot down a simple agenda.

Here's an example:

Client name
Current project or service
Due dates
Additional information needed to complete the service

Doing this will help you to save time looking for project information when you take the call. Plus it forces you to stay focused. You can also use your agenda to "gently" keep your client focused as well. This may seem a bit much but think of it this way. When someone calls you for any reason, they already have an "agenda" of their own even if they haven't written it down. So don't you think you should have your own agenda as well? Give it a try and see how much more efficient your phone conversations become.

One other technique that I use that can really help you with time management is to decide ahead of time how much time you're going to spend on a phone call. This works best when you have a scheduled phone appointment or conference call.

Unfamiliar Numbers

These could potentially be new clients or telemarketers. If you answer and find it's someone inquiring about your products and services, you can save a lot time by having an "elevator speech" already prepared.

This is a short statement that tells a prospective client who you are and what you do. Also having a website that you can direct them to if they're just collecting information can save you a lot of time by not having to explain everything over the phone. Ask him or her to take a look at your website and if they're interested in your services feel free to make an appointment to discuss their needs further.

Calls From Ads

If you run ads for your business, you can save a lot of time by knowing ahead of time where that person learned about you and your business. By using inexpensive tracking numbers, you will know before you even speak to the person calling, where and how they became aware of you. This way you can avoid wasting time asking where they got your number or which ad they got your number from etc.

Instead you will be able to say something like:

"I ran that ad in the Plumbers Weekly specifically to help plumbers like you to get more business."

If you run ads simultaneously in different mediums and for different clientele, how do you know who's calling about what?

The easy way is by using virtual numbers. Basically you will record a message that only you will hear when you get a call from someone. So for the above example you may record:

"Incoming call from Plumbers Weekly"

Right away you will be prepared to address specific needs because you will know ahead of time where they got your information and why they're calling. Here is that list mentioned in the previous section:

FreedomVoice
http://www.freedomvoice.com

Evoice
http://www.evoice.com

HostedNumbers
http://www.hostednumbers.com

How To Stop Procrastinating

There is no magic trick I can give you to stop putting things off. If you procrastinate every now and then, it's not a big deal. We all do it from time to time. If, on the other hand, you've developed a reputation for never getting things done in a timely manner, you've got work to do.

Mindset

First you have to make up your mind to change. Procrastination is a bad habit you have to break. You can change but only if you're willing to put in the effort.

Creating New Habits

The best approach, in my opinion, is to make changes a little bit at a time. You didn't develop the procrastination habit overnight and you won't change overnight. So make small changes consistently over time.

Find Your Personal Breaking Point

A personal breaking point is when something significant to you has to happen to force you to take action and get something done on time. Everyone has one.

For example, I had a friend who would wait until he got a "cut off" notice before he would pay his electric bill. This guy had the money to pay, but he just refused to take care of it for whatever reason. One day he forgot to pay and he arrived home to find his home in total darkness! By the way, it was in the middle of a traditional snowy Chicago winter!

Cold + Darkness = Personal Breaking Point!

He did not like being in the dark and cold. He never waited until the last minute to pay his electric bill after that.

What Happens If You Don't Get It Done?

Think about what will happen if you don't get something done when it comes to your business. What will be the consequences? This is similar to the statement I gave you earlier except now you're making yourself directly responsible. It's a heavier burden to carry if your inability to get things done results in your family not having the things they need to lead a happier life.

It can be different if the consequences include the well-being of others in your life.

The reason some people never try to change bad habits like procrastination is because they haven't had to deal with the consequences. You can't wait until you experience a consequence of not doing something. That could mean the end of your business.

Start Small

Focus on changing your habits by starting with smaller things first. Procrastinators don't just put off things that relate to just one area of their lives. So start with the little things first and build up to bigger and bigger things. If you stay committed to change and stay consistent, you will conquer procrastination and enjoy a lot more success in many areas of your life.

Use Diet & Exercise to Help You Focus Better & Get More Done

How Diet And Exercise Can Help You Focus And Get More Done

In this section you're going to learn the importance of diet and exercise when you work from home. Certain foods can actually give you energy and help clear away the cobwebs when you're trying to focus. You'll also learn which foods can help you be more creative and keep extra pounds from creeping up.

Really? Food Can Help Me Manage My Time Better?

When you eat a diet rich in foods that actually feed your brain, you will begin to notice changes in your ability to focus which means the quality of your work will be better.

Certain foods also elevate your mood, which means you're more likely to work with a positive attitude. That can make a big difference in how you approach even the toughest parts of your business.

There are other ways to revive your tired brain so that you can work more efficiently. This includes regular exercise and additional strategies that can give you the added benefit of taking little work breaks throughout your busy day.

Let's get started!

Simple Ways To Enjoy Better Mental Focus

No matter what type of business you're in, it's so important to take regular mind breaks throughout your day. Your brain gets tired and mental fatigue sets in if you don't take a break.

When you're mentally tired you're literally operating on fumes just trying to finish whatever you're working on. That's also when critical mistakes happen. You may have heard about the German bank employee who fell asleep on his keyboard and accidentally transferred $293 million dollars into an account. The original amount was the equivalent of about $55.00! Ouch!

See what can happen? Imagine if you made certain mistakes in your business. How much time and money could you end up losing?

3 Ways To Stay Mentally Fresh

1. Get plenty of sleep
This doesn't mean that you have to sleep 8 hours a night. Everyone is different and not everyone needs 8 hours. You know better than anyone how much sleep you need in order to function at your best each day. If you're not getting enough sleep due to insomnia, check with your doctor to rule out anything health related. If everything checks out okay with your health, check to see if your nightly routine may be keeping you awake at night. Too much television or caffeine, for example, may be interfering with your sleep patterns.

2. Eat "Happy Carbs!"
I like to refer to certain foods as happy carbs because they don't put you on the emotional roller-coaster ride you get from high sugar foods like soft drinks, cookies, cake etc. Instead go for fruits with a low level of sugar.

Oranges, cherries, grapefruit, apples and grapes are all great choices and will satisfy your sweet tooth. Although they all contain sugar, the fiber in the fruit slows down the absorption of the sugar in your body. So stock up!

3. Eat Protein

Protein produces an amino acid called tryptophan. It is one of the amino acids needed by neurotransmitters to send vital messages to our brains. Unfortunately, our bodies cannot manufacture tryptophan and we must get it from the foods we eat. Soy, lean meat, eggs and dairy are all great sources of protein and aid in getting our neurotransmitters the tryptophan they need. The result is a perkier brain which allows you to get tasks done and maintain greater focus throughout the day.

How To Get More Energy Throughout Your Day

When you work for yourself it requires a lot more energy to get everything done. You're juggling a lot and often under more pressure to bring home the bacon! If your energy isn't up to par, your ability to be productive and get things done on schedule can suffer quite a bit. In this section you'll learn which foods are both healthy and natural energy boosters. Plus you'll learn some other strategies for maintaining energy throughout the work day!

Here is a list of foods that can lift your energy levels and help with productivity!

Energy Boosting Foods

Figs
They taste delicious and are natural energy boosters. You can get the same energizing benefits from both natural and dried figs.

Raisins
Snack on these to jump start your energy levels and they're also natural antioxidants.

Sunflower Seeds
When you're feeling fatigued, snack on some sunflower seeds to give you some much needed energy.

Watermelon
Not only does it taste good but it's good for you! Watermelon is loaded with nutrients and is very low in calories. It's also a known energy booster.

Water
Drink lots of water throughout the day and not only will you have more energy, water helps to cleanse your body of toxins. So drink up! Aim for 8 glasses a day.

Brain Food to Snack On

Almonds
Like most nuts, almonds are loaded with Vitamin E. That makes them great for improving skin, hair and brain power!

Walnuts
Rich in Omega-3 fatty acids, these nuts help you to think clearly and that means less time wasted.

Non-Food Ways to Boost Energy and Your Ability to Think More Clearly

Take a Power Nap
Assuming you are getting enough sleep at night, you might be able receive some real benefit from taking a 20-30 minute nap during your day. The freedom to implement this strategy is one of the great benefits of working from home. You do want to be careful though if you are someone who, instead of a quick power nap, ends up sleeping for hours at a time. This could leave you feeling groggy and less inclined to want to head back into your work routine. Your goal is to feel refreshed and ready to work again!

Take a Short Walk
When you feel your energy waning during the work day, sometimes a brisk walk outside can do wonders. Getting your heart rate up a bit while enjoying the fresh air can have a great impact on clearing your mind and getting your energy level up again.

Meditation
You don't have to be a guru to get the wonderful benefits of meditation. Lots of research has been done on the effects meditation has on the mind and body. Those who meditate daily tend to be able to handle stress better and think more clearly.

Prayer

Many people who engage in prayer daily say that they feel more confident, peaceful and a lot more optimistic, all of which can help to propel your business through the roof!

Visualization Exercises

Athletes like Pro basketball players are taught to visualize every aspect of the game before they play. They hear the crowd in their mind, feel the excitement and energy and see the ball going into the net. Taking a few minutes each morning to visualize the outcome of your day can be a great way to boost your energy and your confidence.

Deep Breathing

When you're feeling mentally drained stop and take 5 slow deep breaths. This will help your body to release tension and provide you with more energy and focus.

3 Ways To Avoid The Dreaded "Work From Home 10"

Ever heard of the "Freshmen 10?" It's the average amount of weight you supposedly gain your first year in college. If you live in the dorms, 3 square meals come with the territory and man do they feed you well! Lots of high starchy foods and sugary treats. Of course there are healthier options but the not so healthy food is also available in abundance. Plus there's a pizza place on almost every corner!

When you begin working from home, it's really easy to get so focused on work and growing your business that exercise just isn't part of the plan. This is especially true if you've never been the type to work out on a regular basis.

When you work for an employer, usually it means commuting to work either by car or public transportation. You may take the stairs and, depending on where you work, you may have a good walk to the office from the parking lot. That's not exactly getting quality exercise but it is certainly better than nothing.

Unless you have an exercise routine in place, working from home can mean your daily commute is 40 feet from your bedroom. It can also mean you spend an extended amount of time just sitting. At least in an office environment you may have to deliver documents, attend meetings and such that allows you to get some form of exercise.

If you're not eating a healthy diet and sitting around for several hours, the pounds can creep up on you before you know it.

Here are some ways to avoid gaining weight while you work from home.

#1 - Plan Your Meals Ahead of Time
One of the best ways to insure that you will be grabbing a lunch and snacks that are healthy during your busy work day, is to be prepared ahead of time. This means allowing time to plan your meals and shop for the groceries that you will need to have on hand.

Prepping healthy veggies and having a good selection of fruit and other healthy snacks ready to go, can really help you to make better choices when you are very busy. Preparation is key when it comes to your healthy diet.

#2 - Get Moving!

Take 30 minutes each day and schedule exercise. You could go for a brisk walk, get on a treadmill, ride a bike, do Yoga, Tai Chi or even lift weights. The key is to just get moving to get your heart pumping and give your muscles a work out.

The benefits in terms of health can be dramatic over time, plus you can lose weight if you need to and avoid putting on extra pounds.

#3 - Stand Up!

Instead of taking phone calls sitting down, stand up and walk around. Even when you're not on the phone, try working while standing. Try taking 5 minute breaks and get up from your desk and walk around your home office. Do some stretching exercises. You can even run or walk in place for a few minutes.

#4 - Get A Trainer

Investing in a personal trainer is a great way to stay in shape. He or she can keep you on track with diet choices and design a workout regimen that will allow you to get fit. It can be really good to have someone else keep you accountable when it comes to diet and exercise.

Exercise Can Help Keep You From Getting Depressed

Going out on your own to work for yourself can be risky and scary for some. Not having a regular paycheck to depend on can cause stress and turn you into an emotional wreck. Next thing you know, you'll find yourself getting way behind on client projects or marketing for new clients because you're feeling emotionally unwell.

A regular exercise routine will keep the blues away because when you exercise your body releases endorphins that make you feel good. When you're feeling good you make better decisions, get more done and are less likely to waste time.

How To Schedule Exercise Into Your Work Day

30 Minutes Is All It Takes!

The most common excuse for not working out is not having enough time to get it done. That's not a reason, it's an excuse. Getting exercise is a must, especially when you work from home.

Unlike people who work outside of the home, your commute is measured in feet and not miles. No long walks from the parking lot to get a bit of exercise. So you're going to have to make time to get it done. Think of it this way, if you're the only one running your business and you don't have a back-up plan, you owe it to yourself and your family to make sure you're getting exercise to increase your chances of staying healthy.

How To Get It Done

A minimum of 30 minutes of exercise each day is the recommended amount to become more fit. In the beginning, try different times of the day to see what feels best for you. If you're a morning person, try scheduling your 30 minutes first thing each morning. You can also work out after quitting time. That's a great way to unwind from the day and clear your head.

Breaks

Schedule a 30 minute break during your work hours to go for a walk. Not only will you feel better, but walking is a great way to spark new ideas and come up with solutions to problems you may be working on. Walking puts you in a naturally relaxed state of mind and allows you to think better. If you can't do 30 minutes, then schedule two 15 minute breaks at different times during your day. You'll still get all the benefits.

Exercise To-Do List

Add exercise to your daily to-do list. When you write it down and make it as important as sending a proposal to a client, you're reinforcing the importance of getting your exercise in each day.

Write it down and really commit to actually following through. If that's not enough to get you to exercise try this.

Write down the consequences of not getting regular exercise and place it where you can see it every day.

Who will provide for your family if your diet and lack of exercise causes a major illness?

If you have children, how will your choices affect their lives?

What if you lose the business you worked so hard to build because you can't work every day?

When you put down what you may lose if you don't take better care of yourself, it can be all the motivation you need to get up and get moving!

Time Management for Work from Home Parents

The Challenge for Parents

Trying to run a business from home with children is tough. After all, raising children is a full-time job too. Although I'm not a parent, I have several friends who work from home and have kids, so for this section of the book I decided to tap their brains a bit to find out how they manage their work time and family time.

The tips and strategies are not in any particular order. I suggest that you read each one and take what works for you in your current situation. What you might find is that even if a particular tip does not address your problem specifically, it may spark some ideas on how to work from home and still enjoy the love and fun of your children.

Tips for Balancing Parenting and Your Business

Many parents run successful businesses out of their homes while also raising happy and healthy children. You can do this too and use the flexibility of having your own schedule to your advantage. It just takes some organization and prioritizing from the beginning to make it work.

How to Get Work Done When You Have Young Children At Home

If you have children who are in school, you'll have to schedule your office hours to coincide with their school hours. That's a no brainer but you should also create an additional "family to-do list" alongside your business to-do list. This way your "work" never interferes with your family time. With so much to get done running your business it's easy to forget that soccer game you promised to attend.

If, on the other hand, you have toddlers at home you've got to have a completely different game plan. Consider hiring a babysitter to watch your kids during working hours. It's not a perfect solution but can go a long way towards giving you the time you need to get your work done.

Toddlers require a lot of attention that you won't be able to give while speaking with a client on the phone. Hiring a babysitter to watch your child can relieve you of a lot of stress and limit the amount of distractions you face while you work.

Schedules

If you have to pick up your kids from school each day, you should add this to your daily schedule. Even though it's a daily event, you should put it on your to-do list because you'll find it easier to schedule work projects around this time during the day. You won't feel stressed out because you have to stop working on something to pick up the kids. You will instead work more efficiently because that time of day is a regular scheduled event, just as writing that new book, working on promotional activities or making phone calls are a part of your regular working day.

What's most important is that you make sure the time you schedule to pick up your kids includes spending time with them. Talk to them about their day and help them with their homework. Decide how much time to allot. It could be an hour, it could be 2 hours. That's up to you. Whatever you decide, make sure that you are always consistent. Kids need consistency, especially from you. It also lets them know that they are a priority in your life.

Outsourcing

In the earlier part of the book on strategies for time management, I included a section on leveraging your time by outsourcing certain tasks. Work from home parents can benefit immensely by hiring virtual assistants. Instead of trying to do everything on your own, you can outsource administrative tasks like bookkeeping, writing business proposals, maintaining updates on your website, graphics and much more. It all depends on how much of your business you feel comfortable handing off to someone else.

Delegating tasks to someone you've hired frees up more of your time to work on client projects, get more business and most importantly to spend more time with your kids. After all, if you're working sun up to sun down, the negative effects on your children can last a lifetime.

Helping Children To Understand That You Are Working

This can be tough especially if you have toddlers. All they know or care about is that Mommy or Daddy is home and available for whatever they need. They don't care about work and don't understand what that means.

You may have to consider working around your toddler's schedule. That may mean getting up very early and working on the most demanding task while they are still asleep. It may be difficult to take calls or place calls with a toddler running around. You could try making calls and answering e-mails during nap time or while your toddler is being entertained by something on television, preferably something fun but also educational.

It's not impossible to run a business when you have very young toddlers in the home, but it will be very challenging. You may have to work on projects later in the evening once your little ones are fast asleep.

Establishing Work Routines For Children

It's a lot easier to teach older children certain rules when you're working from home. Let your children see where you work and explain to them what you do. Answer their questions and allow them to learn as much as they would like to about your work.

Children are proud of their parents and it makes them feel a lot more confident when another child or adult asks them what their parent does for work.

When you let them into your working world they will be more likely to respect the rules about not disturbing you while you are working.

For example:

Instead of telling your kids not to bother you because you're working, tell them you will be working with some really important clients between 3:00PM and 4:00PM or whatever time you decide. Then ask your kids to make a really cool sign that you can hang on the outside of your office door to remind them you're working with clients. They'll get a kick out of making that sign and at the same time they will associate something positive with your work events.

End of The Work Day

Always end your work schedule at the same time each day. Children need to spend time with you and will eagerly anticipate getting to hang out with you. It also shows them that while your work is important, it's not more important than spending time with them. Always be sure to schedule time with your kids and spouse after your work day. Don't go watch television and complain about being too tired to spend time with your kids. Otherwise they will grow to resent your work and may feel they aren't worth your time.

Work Free Weekends

It's really important to maintain focus and get work done during the week. That may mean a late night or two after your kids are asleep. Manage your work time using some of the techniques in this book so that you're not working when you should be spending time with your family. Let the weekends be for family time only. That means no e-mail, no client calls and no work meetings.

You may be a work from home mom or dad but your most important job is being a parent. So never let your business become more important than your children...no exceptions!

Virtual Business & Your Mobile Office

Virtual Business & Your Mobile Office

One of the most amazing things that I've personally experienced as a result of having my own business has been the ability to be completely location independent. Of course this will not be a goal for everyone reading this book, but if the idea of travel or picking up and moving whenever the mood strikes you is appealing, then this section is for you.

If being location independent is one of your main goals in having your own business, you'll obviously need to create a business model that will work for you regardless of where you are physically located. This means that service type businesses that involve location dependent or face-to-face meetings with clients are not going to be the best fit for you.

Certainly there are plenty of service related businesses that can work virtually and, depending on your current skills and interests, could be a great fit for the person who does not want to stay in one place for great lengths of time. Here are some examples: web design, graphic design, SEO, social media management, ghost writing, customer service, virtual coaching and the list goes on.

And if you are in a position to be working 100% for yourself and not be working with clients, you could create niche websites or my favorite recommendation to anyone with a desire to write would be to become a self published author. I consider a writer to be in the best position of all when it comes to taking your work with you anywhere in the world. I can say this from experience as I sit writing this book from an island in Thailand. I made the leap myself and every moment of the freedom I feel has been so worth it.

To begin with, even if you are not quite ready to make that leap to move out of your home or to another country, start thinking about your tech gear and day-to-day business and what it would mean to pack that up to take on the go with you.

Firstly, this will cut down a lot on the amount of physical things that you buy for your business and personal use. You probably want to be able to travel as lightly as possible.

Before I left for Thailand, I had found the perfect computer backpack and this became my "virtual office" while I was still living in the U.S. I made sure it contained everything I'd need for a day out working from Starbucks or various other cafes. I learned exactly what I could eliminate and the types of items I might need to consider adding to my mobile office space.

You'll need to think about things like battery life and power adapters, depending on where you are planning to go and for how long you will typically be without a power source.

You also have many options these days regarding communication online, so even if you are outside of your home country, you can easily keep in touch with family, friends and clients. Skype is a great free tool that can be used for real time instant message, chat or video. There are also additional paid for services that are not very expensive. For example, you can purchase a phone number that people can use to call you without having to dial via another country code. This means that the caller will not incur additional charges and you are able to pick up the call or message via your Skype account.

You can get a free account for Skype here: http://www.skype.com

Only you know what types of gear will be essential for your business as you think about making a big move like this. Begin thinking about it early and enjoy the planning phase and reaching this milestone if it's a dream of yours.

Final Word - It's Up To You Now

I hope that you've found the strategies I've shared with you useful and easy to follow. There's one more thing I want to mention to you. Don't beat yourself up if you don't get your time management skills in order overnight.

Although most of the strategies revealed here were designed to take effect quickly, you may find yourself skipping a day or two. No matter how simple or great the strategies might be, managing time is a new habit you have to build upon.

It all starts with a willingness to change. Once you decide to move forward, you'll be excited and more confident in every area of your life, not just your business.

You can read every strategy over and over again but you have to put them into practice to enjoy the benefits each can provide.

Good luck and I wish you the very best success in business and in life!

Jessica

BOOK 2: START LIVING YOUR DREAM NOW!

How This Book Can Help You Live Your Dream Now!

You purchased this book because you're ready to make major changes in your life. This book can help you begin your journey, but ultimately success will only come if you are willing to put in the time and effort needed in order to live the life of your dreams.

If you're like most people, you spend a lot of time thinking and day-dreaming about living your dream life but that's pretty much where it ends. It's like wanting to drive a car but it's stuck in neutral so you stay parked. Before you can start, you need to figure out what's keeping you from getting what you want in your life.

Learn How To Deal With Self-Made Obstacles

Self-sabotage and all kinds of fears can keep you from doing what you want to do in your life. The first half of this book will go over the most common fears and how to overcome them. Plus you'll learn how to stop sabotaging your efforts so you can get out of your own way and finally live your dream!

Prepare Yourself To Get What You Want

Once you've gone through the sections on fears and self-sabotage, the second half of this book will give you some very easy ways to begin moving toward achieving the life you dream of. The steps you need to take to create a clear path is a lot easier once you acknowledge and actively deal with whatever self-made obstacles you have placed in front of you.

Now let's get started!

Eliminating The Dreaded Dream Assassins

It's enough that we all do things to mess up our own plans when it comes to living our dreams. For one reason or another, we do a lot to block our own success either consciously or subconsciously. One common way we block our own progress is due to the people we choose to allow into our lives. In this section, we're going to take a look at what I like to call the "Dream Assassins" and the role they play in keeping you from living your dreams.

Definition of a Dream Assassin

Dream Assassins are the people in your life who literally make it their career to squash your hopes, dreams, confidence and anything else for that matter. That doesn't necessarily mean these are evil people who wake up every day trying to make your life miserable. I believe a lot of people who do things like this, do so out of habit. It's learned behavior they picked up throughout their own life and to them it may be perfectly normal, believe it or not.

Dream Assassins come in different degrees. Unfortunately, they are often family members, best friends, husbands, wives, boyfriends, girlfriends and others you may have a long standing relationship with. The key to dealing with these types of personalities is to recognize them before they become a problem. In cases where a Dream Assassin has already become a part of your life, there are also ways to deal with them, if you're willing to take the necessary steps that may be a bit awkward and uncomfortable at first. But if you really want to start living your dream you're going to have to deal with them sooner or later. If you allow others to keep you in neutral, you are essentially allowing them and yourself to block your dream.

Dream Assassin #1: "The Mental Blocker Assassin"

What They Do

This dream killer is the kind of person that is constantly telling you all of the reasons why you can't possibly do whatever it is you want to do in your life. They never offer any real facts to back up their theories. They just go on and on, constantly planting self-doubt until you start to believe what they're telling you and before you know it you just give up trying.

For example, suppose someone has decided to get in shape to become a full marathon runner traveling the world even though she has never been a runner before. The Mental Blocker assassin starts telling her how much it takes to run a marathon and that she's too out of shape to even think about attempting to do so. Never mind the probable likelihood that they have never run a marathon themselves.

Why They Do It

This dream killer is usually someone who has dreams of their own that they have never taken steps to fulfill, and they don't want to see you accomplish your life's dream either. It's sad but true.

How To Protect Your Dream

Depending on who this person is in your life you may not be able to cut them out completely. If it's a boss or a close family member, for example, cutting them out may not be the best way to go, unless your relationship is bordering on being abusive.

A simple strategy with this type of person is to stop sharing your dreams with him or her. If they bring up something you've already shared with them, change the subject. If they persist, keep changing the subject. Eventually he or she will "get it" and stop asking. If they persist, just tell them that you've decided not to discuss it any more and instead let the results speak for themselves. Stay firm with this strategy and they will stop asking and move on to another victim.

Dream Assassin #2: "The Yeah We'll See Assassin"

What They Do

This personality type is an extension of the Mental Blocker. They start out seemingly in your corner, rooting you on and encouraging you to go for it. Then it happens. One day out of the blue they start questioning your ability to reach your goal.

For our example, imagine that you tell this type of person that you've decided to go back to school full-time to earn your Masters Degree. Along the way you decide to take fewer courses one semester for whatever reason, but you're still on track to reach your goal. You mention you've decided to take fewer courses to this person and they begin telling you that they knew you weren't going to finish or that they'll believe it when they see it!

Why They Do It

Argh! Usually this type of person has all kinds of personal issues going on. Often they have started on various projects and dreams and as soon as they are within arms reach of getting whatever it is they want, they give up and quit. They feel like a failure and instead of trying again they abandon one dream and start a brand new one expecting a different outcome. But since they tend to do everything the same way, they keep getting the same results.

So, when you mention you're changing your game plan up a bit, they don't recognize that you're simply adjusting plans so that you can increase the odds of getting what you want in your life. Instead, they see you as they see themselves. That is, abandoning the dream only to feel frustrated and disappointed. In other words, they didn't succeed so neither will you. How dare you even think you're going to succeed!

How To Protect Your Dream

Whew! This personality type can really drain you! This is an instance where the advice given for the Mental Blocker can be useful here as well. Stop sharing your dream with them. If it's too late for that, then keep the details to yourself. If at all possible, avoid this type of person. If doing so isn't an option, than you have to be wary of telling them what your own dreams are. Once you know what this person is up to, it's your responsibility to protect your dream.

Dream Assassin #3: "The Don't Dream Too Big Assassin"

What They Do

There are people in your life who really believe that you shouldn't set big goals, and instead, go for and expect less. Usually, this type of personality are people who honestly love and care about you. Often this could be close family members like your parents. It is not their intention to hurt you.

Here's an example. You decide to leave your current job that you've had for several years to pursue something completely different. It doesn't pay as well but you've decided to downsize your life so that you can do what you really want to do and you're excited to get started. You share your dream with a parent and he or she is not so enthusiastic. Instead, they start asking you why you want to walk away from a good job. You're going to have to start all over again. You should do it as a hobby and keep your job because they are afraid that you're dreaming too big and you're going to be unhappy.

Why They Do It

Good loving parents or friends mean well, but they are so afraid of change in their own lives that they freak out when you want to make major changes in your life. They are living vicariously through you. They want the best for you, but they know that they would never leave their jobs to pursue a life long dream. Even if they hate their current job, it pays the bills and puts food on the table. Why mess up a good thing? They see you about to take steps they would never do and it scares them.

How To Protect Your Dream

First, keep in mind that this type of person cares a lot about you and would not do anything to hurt you or mess up your dreams on purpose. They're just afraid for you.

The best way to handle this situation is to stay calm and always be confident when you're discussing what your plans are going forward. The more confident you are, the less afraid they will be. Create some milestones along the way so that they can see how well your plan is working. If you present the changes to them incrementally, it won't feel so overwhelming and it will give them time to accept it a little bit at a time.

At the end of the day, they'll begin to accept that you're making changes and either get on board or not. The more they see you sticking to your guns the quicker they'll come around to accepting the change.

The whole point of these last few sections about "dream assassins" is to help you to understand the importance of surrounding yourself with positive people who will genuinely be in your corner as you make life changing moves. This is your dream we're talking about here! You are the only one who can see it clearly. You are the only one that can make it happen. It will be important for you to have supportive people in your life as you go forward.

In the next sections we're going to focus on self-sabotage and how to stop this behavior from stealing your dreams.

Are Your Sabotaging Your Own Dreams?

There are several reasons why you might not be living your dreams. Some of the most common reasons have to do with fears which are discussed in the next sections along with the steps to take to overcome them. Before you can face fears, you need to understand self-defeating or self-sabotaging behavior and where it comes from.

What is Self-Sabotage?

Self-sabotage is when you deliberately do things to keep yourself from getting from where you are to where you want to be. But why would anyone do anything to keep themselves from living their dreams?

As crazy as it sounds, it happens a lot. It's actually quite normal in an odd kind of way. It's kind of like having a built in protection system that kicks in to "protect you" from feeling the emotions of failing and everything that goes along with that. We all want to get what we want in our lives as long as we don't have to deal with the inevitable failures we may experience along the way, no matter how small they may be. A lot of self-sabotaging behavior also stems from experiences that we had growing up or something someone said that got "stuck" in our thinking.

Let's take a look at some of the most common self-sabotaging behaviors and see if you recognize any in yourself.

Setting Goals That Are Almost Impossible to Reach

Setting a goal that is so unlikely to be reached is a form of self-sabotage.

Here's an example:

Let's say you're working a regular 9 to 5 job making a salary of $50,000 a year. You decide in order to live your dream life, you have a goal to make $200,000 in one year. Now unless you win the lottery, inherit a substantial amount of money, work an additional full-time job or have a small business in addition to your current job, you're not likely to reach that goal in such a short period of time. There is a part of you that knows that it's highly unlikely, but by setting a goal that is not likely to come to pass, you can always tell yourself and the world that you tried but things just didn't work out. This way you don't have to take responsibility for not being able to reach your goal.

Let's take a look at another scenario on the opposite end of the spectrum.

In this example, you set a goal to save money to buy a new car, but instead of creating a budget to reach that goal you spend extra money on things you don't really need. When you're not able to purchase that new car, you tell yourself it's because you don't make enough money, when the real reason has to do entirely with the choices you made.

Here are a few more ways where self-sabotage can keep your dream dangling like a carrot on a stick!

The Not Enough Time Excuse

Another way that you can sabotage your efforts to live your dreams is by claiming that you just don't have enough time to do the things you need to do in order to reach your goals. To make sure that you don't, you allow others to monopolize most of your time. So instead of working on something that will bring you closer to what you want, you opt to go and work on someone else's dream. Not that there's anything wrong with helping someone else, but when you spend the bulk of your free time working on everyone else's dreams, one day you might wake up and realize that your friends have achieved their goals and dreams and you're still just getting started with your own.

Any of the above sound familiar?

Planning Constantly

This one may ring a few bells as it's extremely common when it comes to self-sabotage. You spend a lot of time planning out your dream in every detail. Now that should be a good thing right? The problem is that you never STOP planning. You get right down to the wire, then suddenly you decide nothing about it is right so you start all over again. You never finish because you always need to fix something else and the cycle just keeps repeating itself.

Wrong Place at The Wrong Time

Some people with addictions to alcohol, drugs and even a bad relationship self-sabotage by putting themselves in situations where they are at high risk of giving into the temptation to drink, get high or go back to an abusive relationship. A recovering alcoholic or drug abuser may go to a bar or hang out with friends who use drugs. So if the dream is to live a healthier life free of drugs and alcohol, this would most certainly be a set-up for failure.

So What Does It All Mean?

In every scenario the goal isn't reached because of the behavior. So why do it? That's difficult to say because everyone is different. When you do things to self-sabotage, you do so because you're not aware that you're doing yourself in. You've developed a habitual self-defeating pattern that seems normal so you don't notice there's a problem.

The key to getting on the right track is to create new habits to replace the old self-defeating ones. That's how you begin to take steps to get out of your own way and live your dreams!

The next section offers a simple solution to put a stop to self-sabotage.

Stop Self-Sabotaging Your Own Dreams!

Now that you have a better understanding of what self-sabotage is all about, you need to take steps to stop the behavior.

Step 1: Begin paying closer attention to how you react to situations. For example, let's say that you're trying to get a promotion at work to make more money to put towards your dream. Out of habit you're spending more time chatting with co-workers, playing games on your PC and and other activities instead of putting time into your work. This would be a form of self-sabotage. When you're paying attention to what you're not doing, you can stop the behavior and correct yourself every time until the new habit of focusing on your work dominates your behavior.

Step 2: Don't freak out when things don't go perfectly. Reward yourself when you accomplish something and forgive yourself when you make a mistake.

Step 3: Think about how your behavior may be affecting others in your life. If your dreams includes making things better for your children, for example, check yourself when you choose to engage in behavior that will jeopardize what you want for them as well. Then choose a different action that will bring you and your children closer to the life you want.

In the next section you're going to learn more about what may be keeping you from living your dream and how to rise above it.

The Four Letter Word That Can Stop You From Living Your Dream

That four letter word is...Fear!

We all have fears. Some we are very aware of and others not so much. It's been said that all fears, with the exception of falling, are learned fears. That means that if you have a fear of failure, for example, you weren't born with that fear. You may not get rid of a fear completely, but you can manage it so that it doesn't control your life or keep you from living your dreams.

Acknowledge

The key to getting out of your own way is to first acknowledge your fears. Once you do that, you can take the necessary steps to overcome them. This means having the guts to face your fears head on and deal with them.

In the next sections, you'll learn about the 10 most common fears that might be keeping you from living your dreams. All of them might not apply to your own life, so feel free to go straight to the ones that ring true for you first. If you're not sure, here's a way to know which ones might be an issue for you.

How to Recognize Your Fears

Say each fear out loud 3 times and notice how your body reacts. If, for example, you say "fear of failure" and you feel uncomfortable or there's just something about those words that bother you in some way, that's an indication you may have an issue with failing. You can deny certain things to yourself but your body doesn't lie so pay attention.

We'll start with the fear of failure in the next section.

Fear of Failure

Atychiphobia is the clinical term for the fear of failure. In short, it means having an irrational fear of failing that is so strong within someone that they don't even bother trying to achieve something, even if they want it really bad. This kind of fear can totally block your chances of achieving the dreams that you really do want.

Another important fact about this kind of fear is that failure is a symptom of something bigger. The reality is, fear of failure stems from the feelings of disappointment, embarrassment, shame and hurt when something you've tried doesn't go your way.

Psychologically you attach those feelings to failure. Not surprising. Who wants to feel all of those emotions every single time they fail? So to avoid feeling those emotions you avoid going after anything you have the chance of failing at. Of course that means you pretty much stop trying to do anything and you end up never fully achieving your dreams.

Signs You May Have a Fear of Failure

- You constantly worry about what others think of you.
- Just when you're close to completion of something, you become physically ill.
- You wait until the last minute to finish something which almost guarantees you won't finish a task on time.

How to Change

Embrace your fear.

That may sound odd but if you don't acknowledge it exists, you'll never get to the finish line. By owning up to the fact that you are afraid, on a subconscious level you'll be telling yourself that you're ready to move past your fears. Letting others know can also be helpful. Hearing them encourage you to go for your dreams can be a great boost to your confidence.

Instead of deciding beforehand that you won't be able to succeed at something, make it a point to refocus your thoughts every time you feel yourself falling back on old thinking patterns.

You have developed a habit of expecting to fail. You need to correct that habit by replacing it with a different way of thinking. You won't see results overnight, but if you correct this every time, you will begin to feel differently and changes will soon become your "new normal".

Fear of Success

For many people the "fear of success" just doesn't make sense unless it's your fear. Why on earth would anyone be afraid to succeed?

Well it's not really that simple. Sure, success brings with it a lot of advantages. But just like other fears, it's not that being a success is the problem per se. It's whatever emotional feelings you attach to success that leads to the fear.

For example, if you feel unworthy or uncomfortable in any way when you succeed at something, you may decide on a subconscious level that success equals feelings of unworthiness. Maybe you feel bad because others in your life haven't been so successful and that adds to your anxiety. Or you fear that your friends and family won't treat you the same way.

Can you see how success can become something you don't want?

Add to that the fact that in almost every book you've ever read on how to be successful in life, they state how much hard work, dedication and sacrifices you have to make. Now you have to think about taking risks. It can all be a bit much for some people.

How to Change

Take time to sit and write down what aspects of success bother you the most.

If, for example, you fear losing friends, it may be time to re-examine your current friendships or at the very least your perception of those relationships. Real friends will stick with you through thick and thin. Wishy washy friends will walk away at the first sign of trouble or even when you're doing very well just because they're jealous.

Spend time reading about others who have gone after their dreams and how they dealt with the trappings of success and model how they got through it. Make adjustments along the way and keep moving forward. Eventually you will begin to associate new and healthier feelings with success. The fear may never totally go away but at the very least you can manage it so it doesn't keep you from living the dreams that you envision for yourself.

Fear of The Unknown or Trying Something New

This fear is, in my opinion, so prevalent that you may not be aware it's actually a fear.

Depending on how you were raised culturally, trying something new may not have been something that was looked upon favorably. Since most fears are learned early in life, if not corrected they continue right into adulthood. Parents who are fearful of exposing a child to new situations, people and places, can transfer those fears onto their children.

If you watch the nightly news, the never ending stories about kidnappings, child molestation, bullying and such would make any parent fearful for the welfare of a child. Or if a parent has decided the career that their child should pursue regardless of what the child really wants, this can also lead to a fear of the child changing directions once they become an adult. The programming to only do this and never that has become a part of the child's normal way of thinking.

Have you ever seen young parents scolding a child because he or she wants to touch dirt? A child needs to explore in order to learn, but when you make exploring a negative thing, they learn to fear it. Over time, a child can begin to associate negative feelings and anxiety each time they find themselves being asked to try something different.

As an adult, you may find yourself feeling anxious when your boss wants to promote you. Even if you know a promotion will provide you with the extra cash to put towards something else you want to do, the feelings you've associated with new situations creep in and you will end up subconsciously doing things to avoid or sabotage your promotion.

If this sounds familiar, don't be upset with your parents. They did what they thought was in your best interest at the time.

How To Change

If your fear of trying something new goes way beyond what I've already mentioned here, meaning if you get panic attacks or your mind runs wild with every irrational vision of something catastrophic happening, you should seek the help of a therapist.

If, on the other hand, your fear is more about being hesitant to the point where you're just lacking a bit of confidence in yourself, you most likely will be able to manage your fear on your own.

If living your dream means introducing something completely new, you need to start working on changing a little bit at a time. That doesn't mean you have to necessarily put your dreams on hold. You can work on yourself and work on your dreams at the same time.

Begin right now to make small changes.

For example, if you only eat a particular type of food, plan on going to a restaurant that serves a menu you've never tried before. Try taking a different route home. Go see a movie in a different genre than you're used to. You can work up to bigger and bigger challenges when you feel ready to do so.

It doesn't matter if you don't like the food or the movie. What matters is that you notice that nothing bad happened when you tried something new. Focus on the fun and excitement of getting the opportunity to experience new things. Make it a personal game and soon it will become something you'll look forward to.

Then carry this new freedom forward into the planning of making your dreams and goals a reality.

Fearing You're Not Good Enough

This is a fear that is so common, that it may be the biggest reason so many people fail to even get started towards living their dreams.

Fearing you're not good enough to do or have something is a direct result of negative self-esteem. Chances are that as an adult, no one has called you up and said you're not good enough to be or do anything, but somewhere in your childhood someone did make you feel that way. For some people, they heard it from a parent, a sibling or some other authority figure over and over again until eventually they began to believe it.

For others, it only took one time when they were most vulnerable and it just stuck. In any case, this false belief can stop your dreams dead in their tracks. You may decide you want to pursue an entirely new career from the one you may have now, but you come up with every excuse in the world of why you can't. All of the excuses are to justify your belief that you just don't have what it takes.

How to Change

Right now you have a recording in your mind that is playing the same negative thoughts about you over and over again. You hear it every time you take steps to go for something better in your life.

Starting right now, each time those thoughts that say you're not good enough pop up in your mind…every time you hear the voice of that parent, teacher or whomever saying that you don't have what it takes, I want you to say to yourself...STOP! Then change the thought immediately.

Example:

"I am more than capable of doing what I want in my life."

"It's true that I don't know everything but what I don't know I can learn!"

"I am good enough. I have everything I need to live my dreams!"

The "Wrong Side of The Tracks" Fear

This is really an extension of fearing you're not good enough, but it tends to come up in a different way. Feeling you're not good enough is usually due to bad programming in your mindset. The "wrong side of the tracks" fear tends to apply more in situations where class, social status, education and money come into play. You can be highly intelligent but feel that you don't measure up because you come from a poor background or maybe you lack a certain amount of formal education.

How to Change

You can't change where you come from. It is a part of who you are but that should not be looked upon as a negative. You have a lot to offer the world. Never compare yourself to others and believe that because they have more money or education, they are automatically better than you.

How many times have you watched celebrities with multi-millions of dollars getting arrested?

Take stock in yourself and appreciate what you bring to the table. Don't measure who you are by the amount of money in your bank account. If someone tries to judge you by your background rather than your character, you don't need that person in your life.

If you need to get more education in order to fulfill your dreams, then do so for that reason but not to impress anyone. Never make changes in an attempt to make others accept you. Those kinds of people are not worth trying to impress.

Be true to yourself and watch what happens in your life.

The Fear of Worrying About What Others Will Think

Typically this fear starts way back in childhood. If you grew up in an environment that stressed perfection, for example, you may worry about what others will say or think about you if you make a mistake or fail at something. You may choose goals that you know you're likely to accomplish and never go outside of your comfort zone to avoid having to deal with what others may think.

How to Change

In this case, you've got to make a commitment to yourself to go after your dreams regardless of what anyone else might think. You have to be so focused on your own happiness that what others think about you or what you're doing has no effect on what you do. You don't need to prove anything to anyone.

Take it one day at a time. Choose a day and promise yourself that you're going to do what you want and not care what anyone thinks about it. There's a song by the British artist named Estelle. The lyrics are a perfect example of allowing yourself to be who you are and do what you want to live your dreams regardless of what other think. The song title is "Do My Thing" if you'd like to look that up online.

I'm betting that she does not care what others think about her!

Fear of Being Too Old

At some point in life you may reach a certain age and decide that you need to make a major life change. Many call this a mid-life crisis, particularly if you're a middle-aged man. Male or female it doesn't matter because the fear that you're too old to change or do something different with your life is a self-imposed myth. The only limitations that you have when you're older are the ones that you place on yourself. Of course there may be some physical limitations, although Ernestine Shepherd, the Worlds Oldest Bodybuilder at the young age of 78 would beg to differ with you.

Thanks to advances in medicine, people are living longer and with that many are discovering new careers and coming out of retirement.

You're never too old to live out your dreams. Barring any medical issues, you can start your own business, go back to school, travel the world and just about anything else that you've always wanted to do. But like anything, you have to have the confidence in yourself to create a plan and execute!

How to Change

You've got to work on changing your opinion about your age. Join a social group with members around your own age who are getting out and living life to the fullest. You need to surround yourself with positive people who see life as something to enjoy. Get involved in new activities. Find others in your age group that are doing what you want to do. Ask for advice, learn from them and then schedule time to work towards fulfilling your dreams.

"But What if I Can't" Fears

This is one of the fears that you hear from people who actively sit around coming up with all kinds of reasons why they can't do something. It can be anything as long as it sounds credible enough to their own mind to justify not taking whatever steps are necessary.

How to Change

If this sounds like you, the best advice I can give you is to STOP MAKING EXCUSES for why you're not living your dream. Examine some of the other fears mentioned earlier as you may have more than one fear to deal with. If you don't acknowledge that you are the problem that is keeping you from doing what you really want to do, you will never move forward.

Fear of Rejection

Let's say that your goal is to marry the person of your dreams but you don't go out to social engagements or anywhere to meet new people. Perhaps you choose not to go out because you're afraid of being rejected.

Here's another example…Let's say that you've decided to leave your job and start your own business. In order to make money in your new venture you have to cold call potential clients to try and sell them your product or service, but you refuse to do so because you're afraid of being rejected.

In these scenarios, if you don't make some changes you're going to end up single for the rest of your life and struggling financially because you can't handle rejection.

How to Change

You have to get used to the fact that rejection happens. It's a normal part of life but it's not the end of the world. If you fear rejection you need to desensitize yourself by doing things where rejection can happen. The more you experience rejection, the less power the fear of it will have over you.

You begin to accept that being rejected doesn't mean that there's anything wrong with you. You will realize that you can't control what someone else thinks. You'll begin to understand that most of the time the rejection has little to do with you and more to do with the other person. Over time you will experience more and more confidence as you do everything that you can to bring you closer to realizing your goals and dreams, even taking those risks that could lead to rejection.

Paralyzed by Fear Itself

Probably the most famous line regarding fear has to be one made famous by President Franklin D Roosevelt during his first inaugural address.

He said:

"Let me assert my firm belief that the only thing we have to fear is fear itself...nameless, unreasoning, unjustified terror which paralyzes needed efforts to convert retreat into advance."

Some people walk around in a constant state of fear that literally paralyzes them from taking steps to live out their dreams. They live in a "fear bubble" afraid to do anything, fearing something bad might happen at any time.

How to Change

If this type of situation sounds like you, seek the help of a professional before your fear gets out of hand. Therapy can go a long way towards helping you to cope with irrational fears. A professional can give you techniques to help you and eventually you'll be able to function and see things from a different perspective.

Moving Away From Fears to Planning Your Dream

Hopefully, you now have a better understanding about yourself and your fears. You now have ways to deal with them and not allow the fear to stop you from doing what you want to really do with your life.

Now it's time to take things a step further and really dig into making a plan for achieving your dreams and goals. Having a vision of your dream is great, but you need a roadmap to get you there. The next sections will give you some useful tips and tools to begin putting your plan in place.

Many dreams end up never fulfilled because the "dreamer" never took the time to create a plan to bring what they wanted to fruition.

If you really want to live out your dreams, you've got to have a clear vision of what that dream is. Grab pen and paper and if you have an mp3 recorder or some other way to record your voice that would also be ideal.

The next sections will show you some very simple ways to start visualizing and planning for your dream life...NOW!

How to See Your Dreams Clearly

Congratulations you made it! If you went through the previous sections and identified roadblocks that have been getting in the way of your dreams, you are now ready to focus on the fun stuff!

It's time to sit down and figure out what your dreams are really all about. In order to make your dream a reality, you need to know in as much detail as possible what it is that you want. The more specific you are, the clearer your vision will be. When you have a clear vision of what you want, the steps you need to take to get there also become a lot clearer.

Try this easy exercise.

Look around you right now. It doesn't matter where you are physically...if you're in a room, office or if you're reading this at a local coffee shop. Just look around and observe what you see. Look at the furniture, the layout of the space you're in and the colors. Look at the clothes you're wearing.

Everything you see are all the results of someone's vision. They had to see the end result in detail before one piece of furniture was built, before the layout was created on paper, before the walls were painted. Your clothes were a designer's idea in their mind before one stitch was ever made.

You have to do the same thing with your dream.

In the next sections, I've put together some simple exercises to get you started in the right direction. They will help you to focus on the end results and your initial vision of your dream, not the steps to get there. A clothing designer doesn't visualize stitching a garment. He or she sees what the piece looks like walking down the runway instead.

We'll get to mapping out the details of your dream very soon. For now just have fun and let your imagination do what it does best.

Run wild!

Visualize

When you want to learn the meaning of a word you might look it up in a dictionary or maybe Google it online. Here's an exercise you can do to help you figure out what you really want in your life.

Relax and ask yourself "What is it that I really want?"

Now, imagine that you have a special dictionary. See it as a thick book with thousands of pages. Open it up and begin to flip through the pages and look up your name. Visually thumb through it alphabetically until you reach your page. See a photo of yourself smiling. Now look to the right of your photo.

What do you see?

Where are you?

Where do you live?

What does your home look like?

Are you traveling the world?

Promoted at work?

How much money are you making?

Are friends and family there with you?

Are you working for someone else or for yourself?

Are you happy?

Focus on questions that are relevant to you and whatever it is that you most want.

At this point you will most likely see visual pictures since our brains think in pictures and not words. Just go with what you see.

You only need to spend a few minutes on this exercise. You may find yourself smiling as you watch the pictures going through your mind. That's great! Your body is simply responding the same way it would if what you were watching was real. That's because your brain cannot tell the difference between something that is real vs imagination. After a few minutes, write down what you saw. Throughout the day you may get additional ideas and pictures related to your dream. Just make a mental note or jot them down.

It's a simple exercise that helps you to see what it is that you want in your life without your conscious mind and all of its objections getting in the way.

If you're not the visual type or if you find it difficult to focus in this way the next section takes a different approach.

Write it Down

Take your pen and paper and write down what you want to experience in your life. Not what you think you have to do to get there, just the end results.

Write down the questions listed earlier and feel free to add more if you like. The questions that you ask are going to be directly related to whatever your own desires, goals and dreams are.

Once you have all the questions written down, write your answer to each one. There are no right or wrong answers. This is your dream and all of this should be done without judgment, so don't be concerned right now with what you are writing or what comes up for you during this exercise.

You can be as detailed in your answers as you want to be. Actually, the more details the better.

Record It

Another exercise that works well is to record yourself. Take your list of questions and read them out loud. Then simply answer each question. Pretend you're being interviewed by a reporter. Answer each question in as much detail as you can.

You can answer in the present or future tense. Try both and see how your body and conscious mind responds. If you speak in the present tense but you keep getting conflicting thoughts at the same time, switch to the future tense. It's normal for your mind to put up a mental fight when it doesn't believe what you're saying.

No matter which method you choose to use, in the end you will have a clearer vision of your dreams and future. Use what comes out of this as a source of motivation to propel you forward towards realizing your dreams.

Next, it's time to get your plan down on paper.

You Need a Plan

Now you're going to take the answers you've compiled using one or all of the methods in the previous sections and put them to good use.

It's great to know what you want, but in order to make your dreams a reality you need a plan.

I believe that the reason most people never live the life that they want isn't because they enjoy being unhappy. It's because something is going on in their life that is preventing them from moving forward. They may have one or more of the fears we covered earlier that are keeping them stuck or they spend so much time focusing on the end results that they never get around to creating an actionable plan to actually get what they want.

Here are a few examples of what I mean.

A 2012 survey of 1,400 Americans by the National Foundation for Credit Counseling found that 51% of those polled said that "if" their financial situation improved they would buy a home.

A Gallup pole released in 2013 found that 138 million people from various countries around the world "dream of a life" in the United States.

Toluna PLC surveyed 1,000 Americans and found the majority emphasized the importance of eating healthier but 28% weren't willing to give up their favorite foods, 42% would not give up sweets and 75% said they would not give up poor eating choices unless doing so would make them rich, skinny or loved.

Do you see the pattern here?

In each case there is a want, but what's missing is a plan or the motivation to take what they want from a dream to reality.

You can wish for more money to buy your dream home but unless you've got a magic genie hidden somewhere you have to have a plan to make more money.

All of those 138 million who want to live a dream life in the US had better have a plan in place before they arrive or their dream will most likely become a nightmare pretty quickly.

Knowing one should eat healthier won't do anything unless someone also has the motivation to make actionable positive changes for their health.

Your Dream Plan

Let's take the answers you came up with and use them to create your plan for achieving your dream.

Example:

Let's say you have a dream to become a teacher.

Questions You Might Ask

Q: What grade am I teaching?

A: High school

Q: What subjects?

A: Math

Q: How many students?

A: 20

Now take each answer one by one and write down what you need to do to make that result a reality.

Example:

To become a teacher I need to get my Bachelor's Degree and teaching certification. I will research local colleges and universities to find the best program for me and narrow my choices down to three. I will make appointments to visit each campus, speaking with department heads and career counselors.

I won't go into a lot of detail here as I think you get the idea. Write down as many details as possible. Do this for every answer. Often you will find yourself asking additional questions. That's fine. Just add those additional questions and repeat the exercise over again.

You may not complete this exercise the first time you do it. That really depends on what you want. Someone wanting to fulfill their dream to become a Nurse Practitioner, for example, is going to have a much longer list than someone who wants to become a Yoga instructor. Neither is better than the other. It's personal and specific to you and you alone.

The answers you've written are the basis for your plan. Each answer is like a mini map to point you in the right direction. There's no way that every single step is going to be revealed here. The exercise is meant to give you enough information to get things moving.

Taking Action No Matter What!

You should now have a vision of what you want and it's time to begin working towards achieving your dreams.

Having a vision and a written plan doesn't mean much if you don't take action. If you want to live the life of your dreams, it is at this point where you are at the biggest risk of never achieving that goal. That's because it's at this point where fears begin to creep in and if you haven't dealt with your fears, you're going to have problems trying to move forward.

If you are working on managing your fears or whatever else may be blocking your ability to live your dream life, stay on course. You can work on those while you move forward with your goals.

It is imperative that you begin taking steps no matter how small towards the realization of what you want.

Get Started Right Now

Take a look at your list of answers and choose an area to get started on.

The next section will help you to get going.

Create a Daily To Do List for Achieving Your Dream

1. Choose 3 things that you can do each day to move you closer to your dream.

2. Review what you want daily. Repeat the visualization exercise that you did previously, listen to your recorded session or refer to your written list to keep what you want firmly on your mind. Aim to do this review first thing in the morning and again before bed.

3. At the end of each day write down what you accomplished in terms of working towards your dream. If you didn't get anything done, write down why. If, after a few days, you notice that the reasons that you're not getting something done is the same every time, you need to deal with it asap.

For example, if fear of failure is creeping in, refer back to that section and work through it. Once you are aware of the issue, it's up to you to take steps to manage it.

You're doing all of this to create new habits that will help you to achieve what you want in your life.

Accountability Buddy

Another way to make sure you're taking action towards living your dreams, is to have someone you trust keep you accountable.

An accountability buddy is someone who genuinely cares about you and your dreams. They will help you to stay on track by making sure that you're doing what you said you would do. This partnership works best if both of you are working towards a major goal. That way the two of you can benefit by keeping each other accountable.

Here's a list of some of the things your accountability buddy should do. Of course feel free to create your own list.

- Schedule regular times to meet. Be mindful of your accountability buddy's time. Find a time that works well for them and doesn't interfere with their own plans. Consider meeting once a week. You can meet by phone if in person meetings would pose a problem. If your accountability buddy resides in another city, consider video meetings. Services like Skype are easy to use and will allow you to have face to face meetings without physically leaving home. You can also include email as well.

- Set an agenda before the meeting and set time limits. Use this time to go over what you've worked on and set up new goals to be met before the next meeting.

- Set a beginning and end date. Decide a term between the two of you for when your accountability buddy arrangement will end.

When you have an accountability buddy you'll have someone rooting for you every step of the way. If you have any "Dream Assassins" in your life, your accountability buddy will be a great buffer to help you from being influenced negatively.

How to Maintain Your Momentum

Any dream worth dreaming usually requires hard work, dedication and a lot of motivation to succeed. You've got to keep the momentum towards your dream going until you get to where you want to be.

Here are 3 tips that can help you to do that.

Tip #1 - Stay Optimistic. There are going to be times when you doubt your ability to live out the dreams that you want. That is not the time to quit. Read autobiographies of people who were able to fulfill their dreams in spite of setbacks. Learn why they didn't give up. Study what they did to keep themselves motivated. Find a "hero" and model yourself after that person.

Tip #2 - Refuse to allow others to stop you. Not everyone is comfortable with change and growth. That's their problem. Make a promise to yourself that you will not allow anyone to distract you from your goal.

Tip #3 - When you feel like giving up, go back and remember your visualization exercise. Run those pictures through your mind, seeing yourself living your dream life. Verbally remind yourself how much you want to make this dream become a reality.

Ask yourself why.

Is it so you and your family can lead a better life?

Is it to relieve yourself from the day to day stresses of your 9 to 5 and move to an island in the Caribbean?

What is it that you want so badly that it keeps you up at night?

Recite to yourself why you want what you want and then vow to keeping moving towards realizing your dream.

BOOK 3: THE ART OF DISCIPLINE

How This Book Can Help You

The Art of Discipline will give you some strategies you can start using right now to help you move forward and enjoy a happier more balanced life.

You'll learn some techniques to recognize and pinpoint where your strengths and weaknesses are. Next you'll learn several strategies to help you get rid of old self defeating habits. You'll then use that valuable information to create a solid plan to execute immediately. There's even a 30 day challenge that I think you'll find both fun and rewarding. Finally, you'll learn techniques to make sure you stay on track.

Can All of This Really Change Your Life?

In a word, absolutely! Once you gain the right skills, you will reinvent yourself from the inside out and this will allow you to lead a happier life. Imagine becoming more productive so that you're able to start the business you've always wanted, as an example.

Gaining self-control over your emotions to the point where you no longer react from emotion but from a more focused clear thinking perspective can absolutely be life changing. Can you imagine how much better your life could be?

Here are the tools to help you succeed, but it will be up to you to put them to good use.

Before you can begin building your self-discipline, you should understand a bit more about what discipline is and why it's so important to learn how to use it to your advantage.

Self-Discipline Defined

Self-discipline is all about being able to control your emotions and thinking patterns in a way that allows you to achieve your goals and get a lot more out of your life.

Self-discipline is an ability we all want, but few really know how to attain it. You know you need to make some changes in your life to reach a specific goal or get rid of bad habits that may be standing between you and whatever it is you want in your life. The problem is figuring out where and how to start. The good news is, you are already way ahead of most people.

How is that possible even though you haven't really done anything yet?

The fact that you've purchased this book tells me that you're ready to make some important changes. You're ready to roll up your sleeves and take the necessary steps to learn strategies that will help you get more from yourself and your life.

Why Is It So Difficult to Change?

I think the reason self-discipline is difficult for so many people to even begin to deal with has more to do with what tends to be associated with the word itself. There is nothing positive associated with the word discipline.

Remember what happened whenever you did something wrong as a child? You were disciplined! Put in your place! I won't go on and on because I think you get where I'm going with this. So it's no wonder just the mention of the word brings back not so good associations.

The way to change that perception and take advantage of the positive results that can come from gaining discipline is to discover the good things that are sure to result from putting this into practice.

Let's go back to your childhood. Whenever you decided to "act out" in some way, chances are you were told to calm down and get yourself together. You were told to get a hold of yourself and exercise some self-control.

Really?

Just how were you supposed to do that if no one ever showed you how?

Once you became an adult, the bad habits that you've picked up over the years start to creep back in and it's these habits that keep you from losing those 20lbs, controlling your emotions, getting that job promotion, personal growth and any number of things you want to change in your life.

What You Need In Order to Take Advantage of the Power of Discipline

Understand that self-discipline is a habit that needs to be developed. Once you do so, you can create lasting positive changes in your life. There a few factors that come into play when it comes to building your self-discipline that will help you develop the new habits you'll need to be successful.

Willpower
Some changes you'll make when building the habit of discipline will require a lot of willpower. This is especially true if you're tying to kick a bad habit like smoking or giving up sweets, for example. Even where you may not require a big amount of willpower, you'll still need it to keep you motivated.

Honesty
You will need to be honest with yourself and be willing to acknowledge what your issues are before you can go about initiating real change. If you can admit you have a problem and you're willing to work on yourself, you will be well on your way to better times in your life.

Courage
Change can be scary. It's a general fear of the unknown that causes one to be afraid. It's a normal reaction considering that you're asking yourself to abandon old ways of thinking and adopting a complete new mindset. You'll need to build up your courage and make the decision right from the start to move forward no matter what.

In the next sections, you will learn a few strategies that you can use right now to begin gaining self-discipline in your life.

What You Can Do Right Now to Build Discipline

In later sections, you'll find the most common issues that can be solved when discipline is put into play. There are a number of reasons you may need to work on your self-discipline that are not discussed in this book. But that doesn't mean you can't develop discipline.

Here are a few key strategies you can apply to almost any issue and achieve the results you're looking for.

Excuses

One of the most destructive blows to self-discipline is the constant use of making excuses as to why you can't get something done. For example, things like coming up with excuses on why you can't get to work on time, why you can't save enough money to buy a home, get a degree or start a business etc.

Do you find yourself saying things like:

"Oh I'll register for that class I need to get a promotion at work next semester. I don't have time right now."

"I'll start my diet next week!"

"I'm going to buy that suit and just pay the minimum on my credit cards this month."

When you make excuses for everything instead of moving forward to get things done, you end up not achieving what you want in your life. Even seemingly small things can add up over time.

The way to counteract this is to work on changing the behavior. Every time you find yourself making an excuse for why something can't be done. Ask yourself if that's really true. When you ask yourself for the truth you will be surprised how often you will take a step back and begin to question your own behavior.

Don't let yourself off the hook. Keep asking yourself if your excuses are true. Eventually, you will begin to become more and more uncomfortable each time you make up an excuse. Soon enough you will find yourself wanting to find a solution instead of making excuses.

Control Your Environment

If you've decided on a specific set of goals for yourself, no matter what they may be, you can increase your chances of achieving them by controlling your environment. That means surrounding yourself with others who lead disciplined lives.

You are less likely to lose sight of your goals if your closest friends and people who influence you practice positive self-discipline habits. It's a proven fact that we become more like the people we spend the most time with, so be sure you're spending your time with others who are supportive of your goals and desire to create positive changes in your life.

Become a Student of Persistence

When you are developing your self-discipline, the practice of persistence is extremely important. There will be times when you'll hit a "speed bump" or two that will slow you down. That's where the habit of persistence will come in handy. It is a positive habit that will serve you well over and over again. The best way to practice the habit of persistence is to adopt a "never give up" attitude. Make a promise to yourself to stay focused and always have a back-up plan that you can use to keep moving towards your goal.

In the next section you'll learn how to identify where your weaknesses are so you can focus specifically on areas that need the most help.

How to Figure Out What to Work on First

Self-discipline is something that is needed for pretty much everything in your life that you want to change. Unfortunately there is no way I could possibly list every single area of change.

Instead, I'm going to give you a list of areas that tend to be the most common. This doesn't mean you can't add your own. Everyone is different with different goals. One thing is for sure, no matter what your issues may be. The key to you finding what you need to work on will require you to be brutally honest with yourself.

Let's look at a few examples that will help point you in the right direction.

Weight Loss

If you've ever tried different weight loss plans or purchased any one of a dozen systems from an infomercial but you're still struggling to lose weight, the problem may not be the systems. The exception, of course, is if you're dealing with a health issue that may be hindering your ability to lose weight. If you don't have a health issue, than the reason why you're not losing weight is most likely due to your lack of self-discipline.

Ask yourself a few questions:

Are you eating a healthy diet consistently?

Do you exercise regularly?

Are you following the weight loss system by the book or are you making things up as you go along?

Do you find excuses for not eating a proper diet or working out?

If you're not following the program consistently, that's a strong indication that you need to learn a few discipline techniques to stay on track with your diet and exercise program. It's the only way you'll reach your goal.

Goal Setting

If you're always setting goals for one thing or another but you never quite hit the mark, it could be that you have an issue with self-discipline in the areas of time management and procrastination.

You'll never reach a goal of quitting your job to work for yourself, for example, if you fail to take time to organize your finances and spend time learning about starting and running a business. Instead, your dream just remains a dream until you make the effort to get things rolling.

In this scenario, the way to find out if self-discipline is an issue and the reason you're still just "thinking about" working for yourself ask a few questions.

Do you schedule time every day to work on building your business?

Are you spending money on things you don't really need instead of investing in your business?

Do you look for ways to network with other entrepreneurs or do you avoid doing so?

Hopefully by now you're getting the idea.

Now here is a simple way to figure out what areas of your life you need to work on to build your self-discipline.

Step 1
Take a piece of paper and write down 3 areas in your life you want to improve upon.

Step 2

Now write down exactly the results you want in those areas. For example, if you want to lose weight, write down how many pounds you want to lose and give it a date. If you want to spend more time with your family, write down why you want to spend more time with family and how you'll feel once you reach this goal.

Step 3

Finally, begin asking yourself questions. You can easily come up with questions based on the end results you want. For example, if you want to spend more time with your family here's a few questions you might ask yourself.

What aspects of my current schedule may be interfering with family time?

Am I managing my time so that I'm more productive at work so I won't use up family time to get work done?

What can I do during the week to insure that I have my weekends free to devote more time to my family?

This easy exercise will accomplish two things for you. First, you'll force yourself to focus on what's really important to you right now. Second, by asking questions you are revealing specific areas you need to exercise better self-discipline in order to get what you want.

In the next section, you will take the information you've just gathered and use it to create a daily plan to help you build more discipline into your life.

How to Create a Simple But Powerful Daily Success Plan

In the last section you learned some easy ways to identify where and how to focus on areas you need the most help with. Now you need a plan. A "road map" to keep you on track from one day to the next.

Here's an example to put this in perspective. Thirty years ago if you needed to get directions to a city you had never visited before, the most common way to find out how to get there would be to purchase a road map and plan your trip.

Today, hardly anyone uses old fashioned road maps anymore. Now GPS in cars and on smart phones do all of the work for you. You just give it the address and you're good to go.

The methods in these examples to get to the destination are very different but the results are the same. Keeping that in mind, don't worry if one strategy here doesn't work for you. Try as many as you need to and eventually you'll find one or more that will be the best fit for you.

Creating Your Daily Success Plan

I suggest creating a daily success plan, because in order to become a master of self-discipline you will need to work on yourself daily. Gaining better self-discipline in any area of your life means that you will be working on changing the way you do things, changing your mindset and developing new habits.

Never Underestimate the Power of Simplicity!

You can enjoy amazing results in your life without making everything overly complicated. When the plan is easy you're less likely to be overwhelmed and quit. That doesn't mean you won't have missteps along the way.

What you need to keep in mind is that you are the ultimate key to success and change when it comes to self-discipline. Once you understand that all of the control is within your own power, you can change your life for the better.

Creating Your Simple Daily Plan

If you've completed the exercises in the previous section, hopefully you've identified what you need to work on. Now you're ready to make self-discipline work for you.

Your daily plan will consist of 3 steps that you'll carry out each day based on the areas you decide to focus on.

Here's where your willpower, honesty and courage are going to be important factors. If you need to, go back to that section and re-read it. You will need all of those factors in place before you move forward.

Step 1 - Start your day with a list of 3 things that you can do that will bring you closer to whatever goal or situation you're looking to improve.

Step 2 - Carry your list with you throughout the day and refer to it often. This will force you to be more accountable for the actions you take or don't take in relation to the areas you're working on in your life.

Step 3 - At the end of each day go back to your list and check off each completed task. If there are tasks you did not complete, don't freak out! Save the list and make a new one for the following day and repeat the steps.

You can do this every day of the week. At the end of the week, look over each day and see which tasks you completed and which one you did not. Then take a sheet of paper and draw a line down the middle. On the left side at the top of that column write, "Things I Completed" and on the other side write "Things I Did Not Complete".

Now take a look at the tasks you did not complete. Is there a pattern?

For example, let's say one of your goals is to lose 20 lbs so you wrote down that you would not eat fast food. On 3 different days you did eat at your favorite fast food restaurant. That is an indication that your self-discipline needs work in terms of willpower. Remind yourself of how important it is to lose those 20lbs.

Remind yourself why you want to lose the weight. Then think about how good you're going to feel when you achieve that goal. This exercise is a great way to nudge your mindset into making you more focused and accountable so you will want to exercise more discipline in that area. You will begin to associate something positive with discipline because of the end result you will achieve.

Now look at the list of tasks you did complete and give yourself a pat on the back. Use the positive aspects and feelings you get from sticking to your guns and using your willpower to get what you want to further move you closer to mastering the art of self-discipline.

Next, we'll take a look at some of the most common areas of improvement and how to change for the better.

The Most Common Problems Solved by Gaining Discipline

The previous sections focused more on general strategies for building your self -discipline.

In the next 5 sections you'll learn how to deal with some of the most common issues along with specific strategies for each.

The areas covered are:

Weight Loss
Anger Management
Financial Management
Relationships
Procrastination

If any of the above issues are relevant to your life, you can go right to that section and get started. Even if your specific issue isn't listed you can still use the strategy and apply it accordingly.

How to Prepare

Be sure to ask yourself questions to help you identify what you need to work on.

Be Open to Change

The more you work on yourself, the easier change will become. Allow yourself to be open to the changes and soon you will begin to experience positive results in your life. Mastering self-discipline takes time and dedication so make a promise to yourself to put your best foot forward. You'll enjoy the results for many years to come.

Let's get started with the issue of weight loss.

Self-Discipline for Weight Loss

In an earlier section, we used weight loss as an example. At any given time millions of Americans are on some kind of diet trying to lose weight. It's why the diet industry is a multi-billion dollar a year industry and there's no sign of that number decreasing anytime soon. That's because we're looking for that "quick fix" solution to losing weight. That's why 85% of those trying to lose weight end up giving up early in the process.

If this sounds familiar, you can increase your own chances of losing the weight you want by adding a self-discipline technique to help.

Based on what you've already learned about discipline, figure out what areas you need to work on in order to succeed. In most cases a lack of willpower is the culprit that derails your weight loss goals.

How to Tap Into Your Willpower

You know the story. You start out excited and finally ready to drop some pounds. You start out eating the right foods and exercising 5 - 6 days a week.

Maybe a week or two into your diet and exercise program you begin eating bad foods that put on more pounds. Eventually, you don't even bother working out or you cut back on it until you're not exercising at all. Then you complain to anyone who will listen how tough it is to lose weight.

What's happening here?

That's easy. You've got to give your willpower a tune up and you've got to control your mindset.

If you try to correct yourself by focusing only on the foods you're not supposed to eat, you'll end up failing miserably. That's because you're giving a lot of energy and thought to the very thing that is holding you back.

Instead, focus on seeing yourself at the weight you want. Think about the activities you can participate in when you weigh less. See yourself wearing the clothes you'll get to wear and the looks you'll get in admiration from others.

Go ahead and let your mind enjoy this vision. Do this exercise every time you feel tempted to eat something you should not or when you want to skip your work out.

This is where your willpower comes in. It's going to be easier to avoid doing things that will keep you from reaching your weight loss goal. Your willpower will kick in and literally remind you of the consequences if you give up.

Do this every single time you feel tempted and eventually this new way of dealing with food cravings and such will become habit. Early on in the process your willpower may let you down. It's normal. It happens. Just reset and go through the steps again.

Self-Discipline for Anger Management

Recently a famous singer was diagnosed as bi-polar and suffering from post traumatic stress syndrome. This diagnosis explained some of his frequent and over the top responses to various situations with out of control anger and physical reactions. In his case, his anger issues may not be fully controlled by willpower alone. He will most likely have to be placed on medication.

Unless you've been diagnosed with a mental disorder that prevents you from controlling your emotions, you are responsible for the consequences of your choices.

Self-discipline is the best way to keep your anger under control. Instead of lashing out when something or someone "pushes your buttons" you can learn to handle the situation better.

How to Use Discipline to Control Your Anger

In order to discipline yourself not to lose control and let anger take over, you have to learn and understand why you get angry in the first place. Psychologists believe that the reason some people erupt, overreact and lose control over seemingly harmless things is due to perception and fear.

For example:

You think someone is putting you down when they offer to help you do a specific task. In your mind they're not trying to help you. Instead, they're just trying to make you look bad.

Another point worth mentioning is that when some people lash out in anger over something minor, the "fight or flight" response we all have when we're in danger kicks in. Even if someone is not in danger, their mind perceives the situation as fear and so they may react and appear over the top to others.

How to Discipline Your Mind to Control Anger Outbursts

There are so many reasons why your anger might be out of control as one's "anger trigger" can be different from one person to the next.

If your anger is so extreme that you are causing physical harm or verbal abuse to yourself or others please seek professional help.

If, on the other hand, you're just known for flying off the handle or you're described as being a bit too sensitive, you can take steps to get a handle on your anger using self-discipline strategies.

In this case, willpower doesn't usually work so well. That's because out of control anger stems from false beliefs or incorrect perceptions. So you have to start with your mindset.

Each time you find yourself getting worked up over something, stop and focus on what you're thinking about in the moment.

Ask yourself a question.

Why am I getting angry?

What's going on here that has me losing control?

Then every time you find yourself getting overly angry about something go through this exercise. You will soon begin to notice a pattern.

Let's look at the example of someone who gets upset when their work is questioned, even if it's a routine question anyone might be asked. Perhaps for this person, there was a time in his life when someone questioned his work and it made him angry. So now when he finds himself in that same scenario, he assumes everyone is doubting his ability to do the work well, even if that's not the case.

Your mind can play the same scenario over and over again causing you to feel the negative emotions associated with it.

Now that you know where that anger stems from, the next time you find yourself getting angry you can stop yourself from losing control.

You want to change the scene that is playing in your mind. See yourself reacting rationally and calmly. Mentally tell yourself to stop, slow down and respond in a controlled manner. It takes time and a lot of practice but if you're consistent you will see positive results.

Self-Discipline for Financial Problems

Do you find yourself constantly complaining about not having enough money to buy the things you want or maybe you're always struggling to cover your bills every month? Perhaps you want to save up to buy a new car or home but you find yourself dipping into your savings to pay for other things. It can seem like you're on a treadmill that never stops.

When it comes to dealing with financial issues, the reasons you don't have the money you need could be from circumstances out of your control. This might be the case if you're laid off from your job or if your health is compromised to the point where you are unable to work.

In those situations, it's not about self-discipline. For our purposes here, we're going to assume that you're either getting a steady paycheck working for someone else or that you are bringing in steady income working for yourself.

Let's say you want to save money for a new car because your current car is on its last leg. Instead of setting money aside from each paycheck to put towards a down payment on a new car, you go and buy things you don't really need. Or you spend money entertaining family and friends paying for lunches and dinners.

You get to the end of the month and that's when reality sets in. You add up how much money you've spent on miscellaneous items and you're surprised at the high amount you've spent.

Often times, when the next month rolls around you end up repeating the same behavior. If you continue on this path, you'll end up driving your old beat up car, wasting hundreds of dollars trying to keep it running.

How to Use Self-Discipline to Help You Financially

Whether you're tying to save up for a major purchase, retirement or just to build up a nest egg, you can do it no matter how much or how little you make.

There are a lot of people who make what most would consider low incomes but somehow still manage to put their kids through college, buy a home and retire comfortably.

Compare that to those who may make upwards of six figures but still struggle to pay off student loans from 15 years ago and have credit card debt up to their eyeballs.

How is that possible?

The answer is simple. It's all about self-discipline. It's not the amount of money you take home, it's what you do with the money that makes all the difference.

If you're spending your money instead of saving and investing a percentage of it regularly, you'll never achieve what you want financially until you adopt some habits in self-control. You have to discipline your spending habits.

First, decide what your financial goals are. Do you want to save to purchase something specific? Maybe you want to save a certain amount of money each month for a down payment on a house. Whatever it is, write it down.

When you take the time to write it down you are subconsciously telling yourself that what you want is important.

Then write next to each item why you want to buy a car, a house, save a specific amount of money or whatever those financial goals are for you.

Maybe you want to invest your savings to pay for your children to attend college. Maybe you want a bigger home in a better neighborhood or you want to travel around the world.

Then write down how you will feel when you reach your financial goal. When you attach emotions to the goals, they can take on a different meaning and you'll be more likely to stick to your plan.

Keep that information where you can see it every day. Every time you decide to spend money on something frivolous you will stop and think about why you're trying to save money.

Thinking about the better life a college education will give your children can stop you from making poor financial decisions as an example.

Self-Discipline for Better Relationships

Our world revolves around the relationships we have with our spouse, love interest, co-workers, boss, teachers, our children, family and friends. When there is a lack of self-discipline in the area of relationships it can become a major problem.

To cover all of the mentioned relationships goes beyond the scope of this book, so I'll focus on the most common issues.

Couples. Either married or just dating, it doesn't matter. Problems you have with your significant other are typically a result of deeper issues. These might include such things as cheating, emotional or physical abuse or trust issues, as examples.

Reoccurring issues can be avoided or stopped completely by developing new habits of self-control.

Also, if you are in an abusive relationship, you should seek professional help.

How Self-Discipline Can Improve Your Relationships

Sometimes people move from one relationship to the next but often find the new relationship is just as bad as the last one That's because until one deals with why they are allowing the same kind of personality into their life nothing will change. Again, as in the other examples, you can start working on change by asking yourself a series of questions to get to the root of the problem.

Example:

If you have a roving eye and routinely cheat on your partner, you need to be honest with yourself and question what you do over and over again. Ask yourself if hurting the person you claim to love is okay with you. Are you prepared to lose the one you love?

Think about the consequences of your actions.

The next time you have the opportunity to cheat, stop for a second and think about the answers to the questions. Willpower is going to play a tremendous part in this example for obvious reasons.

Cheating in a relationship stems from something much deeper that may have nothing to do with your spouse or significant other, but for whatever reason you're choosing to cheat as a way to deal with whatever the real problem may be. Therapy can do a lot to help you figure it all out.

In terms of willpower, it will take a lot on your part to change. It may take a good amount of time to change. Unfortunately, the type of self-discipline needed is tough but not impossible. It may all boil down to the importance you attach to the change. You have to want it and be willing to do whatever is necessary to save your relationship.

Self-Discipline for Procrastination

Can you imagine what would happen if everyone could develop self-discipline in the area of procrastination and time management? So many things in our world could change if we all were a lot more disciplined with getting things done in a timely manner.

If procrastination is a problem for you, the positive results you can enjoy from gaining discipline in this area will seem like magic! Imagine you're not wasting time, you get more done each day and maybe for the first time in your life you actually "value" time.

Disciplining yourself in this area is about developing new habits. So if, for instance, you're known for always being late, you can discipline yourself to change this behavior.

Something else to think about when it comes to dealing with procrastination is that you'll find other habits related to time management will also improve as you gain strength in this area.

How to Discipline Yourself to Eliminate Procrastination

First you have to admit that you have a problem with getting things done on time. Acknowledgment can open up your mind to being more motivated to change.

Then explore why you wait until the last minute to get something done.

Remember, discipline in any form is simply a habit. Procrastination is just another habit that needs to change in your life.

To do this, you need to take it one step at a time and not try to change too much at once. Otherwise you may become overwhelmed and slip right back into your old habits. Choose one aspect of your procrastination habit and focus your energy there.

As an example, let's say you want to arrive on time to events and get to work on time.

Come up with a series of small ways to manage your time better.

You might set your smartphone or PC calendar to remind you to get ready to leave or finish a work project so that you can make it to an appointment or event on time. Then make it a point to leave at the scheduled time. Do this over and over again and soon you won't need to rely on constant reminders.

Once you get the hang of it, you can move on to other issues related to procrastination.

If you find yourself resistant to change, you need to spend time learning why. If you don't, you'll never be able to change your time management issues and they will continue to cause problems in your life.

The Self-Discipline 30 Day Challenge!

Change can take time but the rewards for doing so can make your life a new and exciting adventure.

Gaining self-discipline can open doors to new opportunities and allow you to lead a happier, balanced life. Building self-discipline is a process and it should be something you commit time and effort to in the long term.

No matter how much positive growth you manage to achieve there's always room for more.

Getting Started With The 30 Day Self-Discipline Challenge

How It Works

Each day for 30 days you will focus on one area to build your self-discipline or to reinforce a new habit you've developed already. This will allow you to work on areas where you're the weakest. This kind of challenge can also be a lot of fun.

At the end of the 30 days you'll be able to measure your progress by the changes you experience throughout the 30 days. You choose the area to work on because your habits and the changes you need to make are unique to you.

How to Prepare For The 30 Day Challenge

Purchase a journal or a simple notebook.

If you've gone through the previous sections, you should have a pretty good idea of what you need to work on to gain better discipline. For the challenge, you're going to choose one thing to work on.

Let's say that you choose procrastination.

Every day for 30 days you're going to do something that helps you eliminate activities that lead to procrastination. In your notebook or journal each morning before you get on with your day you will choose one thing to focus on for that day. Then you'll also write why it's important to do whatever it is you choose to focus on that day.

Example:

Day One - Today I will focus on making sure I stay productive at work and complete my work projects in an orderly manner. The reason I want to be productive is because it will make me a better employee and may eventually lead to a promotion and a higher salary.

Then right before you go to bed you will record whether or not you achieved the goal for the day. Congratulate yourself if you did. If you did not achieve your goal, write down why you believe you missed the mark and how you plan to do better the next day.

You'll do this every single day for 30 days.

In the beginning it will require more effort on your part because it's natural for your mind to resist change. If you stick with it, you will develop a new positive habit that will eliminate procrastination for the long-term.

What's cool about this 30 Day Challenge is that you can repeat the process as many times as you like until you get the results you're looking for.

Although it's virtually impossible to list every single self-discipline habit and area of improvement, here is a list of 30 day challenge ideas to help get you started.

Weight Loss
- No processed sugar
- Drink 8 glasses of water
- 30 minutes of cardio
- No meat

Procrastination
- Be on time for work or school
- Complete one task each day to get closer to starting your own business
- Complete work projects each day and do not bring work home

Financial
- Take your lunch to work instead of buying lunch
- Take the $5 you use to buy coffee each morning and add it to your savings instead
- Take public transportation and donate the money you save on gas that month to charity

Get the idea?

Challenging yourself to change for the better can be extremely rewarding and fun!

Reward Yourself

Before you begin your Self-Discipline 30 Day Challenge, think about a way to reward yourself for a job well done. Just make sure the reward doesn't contradict what you worked so hard on during the month.

In other words, if you complete 30 days with no sugar, don't reward yourself with a large apple pie and your favorite soft drink. Instead, go for something a lot smaller that won't send you into a wild and crazy sugar binge.

How to Keep Your Momentum Going

Once you've completed your first 30 day challenge you can choose to try a new challenge to reinforce your new positive habit. Or you can choose an entirely new challenge in another area that you feel you need to work on. Either way you will be reprogramming your mindset, boosting your ability to stay motivated and creating a new improved you with a brand new set of life changing self-disciplined habits.

Have fun with this!

BOOK 4: YOUR ORGANIZED HOME

Decluttering Your Environment

It's amazing how quickly "things" can accumulate in our environment. Maybe it's because life gets in the way and before you know it, you've got clutter!

It may also have a lot to do with familiarity and comfort that makes throwing something away very difficult for some. It's like having a big old comfy chair that may be old, worn out and way too big for the room. But no matter how bad it looks compared to everything else in the room, you love that chair and it's not going anywhere!

Chances are that you associate a lot of memories with it as well. If, for example, it was the first piece of furniture you bought when you moved into your first home or apartment, it could have a lot of sentimental value. The thought of getting rid of it just might not be an option for you.

The key to making your environment work with you instead of against you is to organize. If you're not organized, that's where trouble can start. It's not that you don't want to get things in order. It's more about having a simple system that is realistic so that you won't feel overwhelmed by the process.

The Benefits of a Clutter Free Home

You may not realize just how much clutter has become a problem in your life until you can't find those important tax documents or you can't find room to display your prized collection of first edition books. The benefits of keeping your home clutter free are obvious.

- When you're better organized you won't waste valuable time looking for things.

- Creating a new habit where you store items according to a system means you're less likely to have clutter issues in the future.

- An organized home will allow your decor style to shine through.

In the next sections of this book you're going to learn some very easy ways to organize the different rooms in your home. There is also a bonus sections about re-purposing old items.

Prepare Yourself

Now before you dive in, you'll need to prepare yourself. The reason many people end up giving up long before the job of organizing their home is complete is because they didn't take the time to prepare.

Decluttering your home, like anything else that requires time and effort, requires a plan.

Imagine walking into your bedroom with piles and piles of books, clothes and boxes everywhere.

Without a plan, you'll end up standing in the middle of your room thinking about how you're going to get rid of everything. Within minutes you'll begin to come up with reasons why you can't organize anything and decide to try again some other time. Only some other time almost never happens.

Now let's change the scenario up a bit.

Imagine you are walking into that same room, but this time you've already taken an initial inventory of everything you have to deal with and have a written plan of how to get rid of the clutter. Not only that, but you even have a set time period to start and end your project.

Can you see what a big difference just a little bit of planning can do?

How to Create Your Organization Plan

Grab a pen and paper. You don't need anything that's overly complicated here. The reason you should write it down is because when you do so, your mind almost automatically gives it a higher level of importance. That means that you're more likely than not to execute your plan.

1 - Title your page "My Declutter To Do List"

2 - Pick the area of your home that you want to work on. I suggest sticking to one room or area at a time.

3 - Go to the room or area you've chosen and take an initial inventory. That means scanning the room and writing down what needs to be done in order to get that room organized. If, for example, your room has way too many knick knacks and other collectibles giving it a "junky" kind of look, let that be your main focus for that particular room. There may be other things that need to be done, but instead of trying to do it all at once, schedule another day to tackle those issues.

4 - Schedule the time to work. Simply block out whatever amount of time you feel comfortable with. The most important thing is to commit to sticking to it and following through. Don't schedule 3 hours unless you honestly believe that you're going to stick to it. Otherwise you may get down on yourself for not hanging in there and abandon the project. Don't schedule another day or room until you've finished your first room.

5 - Get family or friends to help you if the job is too big for you to handle alone.

6 - Gather any necessary supplies. Depending on what needs to be done, you may need the following:

- Storage bins
- Garbage bags
- Cleaning supplies
- Tools
- Tape

Additionally, make sure that you have the following items:

- A set of colored markers.
- Different colored sticky notes (large or small size)
- Clip board
- Blank paper
- Patience and a positive attitude!

Now you're ready to get started. Let's move on to the next section.

Ready! Set! Organize! - Get it Done the Easy Way!

No matter what part of your home is in need of organizing, this simple system will work wonders for you if you are ready to stick to the plan.

About 99% of the time, when you decide to get organized it's going to also mean getting rid of things you've been holding onto for years. If you're ready to do that, then you're ready to finally get rid of clutter and organize your home.

How To Get it Done!

1 - Take three sheets of paper and 3 colored markers, one red, one green and one blue. On the first sheet of paper use the green marker and write in large letters the words "Let it Go". On another sheet of paper, with the red marker write "Keep" and use the blue marker to write the word "Donate" on the third sheet of paper.

2 - Now take each sheet and tape them to an available wall or if you don't have the wall space, you can place them on the floor instead. Just space each page out so that you have three separate areas.

3 - Before you can begin the process, you need to be clear about what should go where. Let's take a quick look at each one of the sheets of paper that you just created.

Green Marker - Let it Go

Green means go! Move on! Get out! So anything you place in this section is going in the trash. You will need to decide what items get thrown out. An easy way to determine what ends up in this section is to ask yourself a few questions.

- How long have you had it?

- If it's clothing, when was the last time you wore it?

- Why are you still holding on to it?

- If it's mechanical, does it still work as it should?

Hopefully you get the idea here. If there's no logical reason to hold on to the item it's time to *let it go* and send it to the trash.

Red Marker - Keep

These are items you've decided to keep. Usually important items like tax files, insurance papers, photos etc end up in this section. It can also contain items that have some kind of sentimental value to you. In that case, only you can assess it's value and importance.

Blue Marker - Donate

This section is self-explanatory. You may have items that are in great shape but you just don't need them any more. That makes them great items to donate to charity or give away to family and friends.

The questions you ask yourself and the answers you get will also determine where the item should be placed. So you don't really have to stand in the middle of your room all day talking to yourself!

If, for example, you come across an old pair of jeans, ask yourself how long it's been since you last wore them. Let's say you decide you don't need to keep those for yourself but they're still in wearable condition. You may then decide to place them in the "Donate" section instead of throwing them out.

You may also find that you don't need to go through each step for every single item as some items will either obviously need to be thrown out or the item will be something that you know you wish to keep and you don't need to ask yourself any questions.

You can also opt to use colored sticky notes instead. That's really up to you. I included them just as an option.

What To Do Next

Once you've organized your items using the method above, you can deal with each section accordingly.

Start with the "Let it Go" section and dispose of those items immediately. The sooner you do so, the less likely you are to go through the items again changing your mind.

Next, arrange to have the items marked for donation to be picked up or dropped off.

Finally, you'll go back to your red pile and put those items away.

In the next several sections you will be able to use this simple system to organize every room in your home. Don't worry if you're trying to figure out what to do with all of those "Keep" items. I've included some great storage ideas in this guide as well.

What's most important about this system is that it allows you to see what you're dealing with so that you can see the light at the end of the organizing tunnel. It makes it a lot easier to then continue the process.

Once you've completed these steps, you can rearrange the remaining items and tidy up where needed.

Finally, you'll choose a storage system that works best for a particular room to help you maintain your new organized space in the future.

Organizing From Room to Room

Now that you have a system in place it's time to get busy. In the next sections it's all about organizing from room to room. Feel free to check out each section or just go right to the room or area that you're most interested in getting organized first.

In each section, you'll find tips that you can use right away to organize your space as well as additional tips for keeping it that way.

The rooms covered are:

- Living Room/Dining Room
- Home Office
- Bedroom
- Bathroom
- Kitchen
- Garage
- Closets
- Kid's Room

I've also included a section on storage solutions for all those items that you want keep or display.

If you're on a budget, you're going to love the section on how to re-purpose old items and turn them into storage bins with a decorative twist.

Remember, you're going to use the organizing system outlined in the previous section. So be sure to have your supplies and other tools ready before you get started.

The tips provided are general by design due to the fact that every room and every home is different. So you will have to improvise based on your own situation. The tips are designed to spark some ideas that you can use based on your own style, decor and room size.

In each section, you'll find valuable tips and solutions for the most common problems in that particular type of room.

You'll also learn about some of the best storage options that are stylish and easy to install options for keeping your room organized. They are all easy to implement and might also help you come up with your own ideas along the way.

Let's get started!

Living Room/Dining Room

Challenges

Probably the biggest challenge you'll run into with the living and dining rooms is that they are often one of the busiest areas of a home, with the kitchen arguably the busiest. These rooms seem to take on many functions.

It's where family members and friends gather to socialize and eat meals. Unless there is an additional room designated as a separate family room, the living and dining rooms take on additional roles as the center for entertainment where everyone watches television and plays video games, among other things.

Sometimes these areas will also double as a makeshift home office.

With so many different activities taking place, it's no wonder living rooms end up in need of some serious organizing.

Solution

If this is a scenario that sounds familiar, you need to sit down and "rethink" your rooms.

If your living room is considered average in terms of size, you're probably trying to cram a lot into a space that seems to get smaller as you add more items. One way to tackle organizing your living room is to first decide if there is any activity that can be moved to another room in your home. This will immediately free up space.

If the dining room is turning into a lot more than just the place where meals are enjoyed, you may need to reclaim that room completely. Meaning it may better to designate that room as a place for having meals only.

Or think about rearranging the space so that it is more suitable as a multi-function room. You can do that by organizing one area for meals and another area for your home office. Just be careful not to fill the room with unnecessary items.

Use the system you've learned here to decide what gets to stay and what goes. Do this regularly to keep your room organized long-term.

Additionally, you can take steps to get more space by simply looking for "hidden" places you may not have thought about before.

Here are a few ideas:

If your sofa is currently right up against a wall, try moving it away from the wall creating another little space. Of course this will only work if your living room is big enough to do so. You don't have to create a tremendous amount of space to make this work. Start with about one foot from the wall. Now you have an extra little area to store some things. Placing items in storage bins will keep it looking nice and tidy. Just try not to stack bins so high that they are visible. Let the couch "hide" your secret storage area.

If your living room is overrun with video games, the family computer, books and other items, consider purchasing a storage cabinet that matches your decor and will hold all of those items. This allows you to keep track of everything and keep them all organized at the same time.

Magazines, Mail & Newspapers

Anything made of paper tends to end up laying around and piling up pretty quickly. Create a central area in your living room where these kinds of items can be stored. You can purchase storage bins made specifically to hold and display magazines and other paper items. At the end of each week make it a habit to go through the bin and throw out old newspapers and other items that are no longer needed.

Photos

Photos on your wall are wonderful and add a lot of warmth to a living room. The problem is that when you have too many photos it can create a very cluttered look. If you have a lot of pictures on your walls, consider reducing them. There's no magic number here, you'll have to figure that one out. It would be even better to have someone else, like a family member or friend, to give you some input. Sometimes when we're too close to something we can't see what other can.

You could also purchase picture frames that have several frame shape cut-outs. So instead of just one picture you could have a dozen but with only one frame to hang you'll reclaim quite a bit of wall space.

Collections

If you're a collector of most anything that can be placed on display in a home, it's tempting to want to place every collection somewhere in your living room.

I have a friend who has a huge coffee mug collection. Many of them are over-sized and take up a lot of space. He has them in the kitchen and all over the living room.

If you have a lot of collectibles in your living room, no matter how great they may be, too much of anything just makes the room look cluttered.

Instead, considering placing a few of your collectibles on display and carefully packing the remaining ones in a safe place. Plus, if your collections are valuable, it's always best to keep them in a secure place where you can lower the risk of theft or damage.

Additional Tips to Stay Organized

Look at your current furniture and see if anything can double as a storage source. Is there room underneath your sofa? How about your cocktail table? If you're in the market for a new set of furniture, look for something that has additional hidden storage built right in.

Home Office

For this section I'm going to add some additional steps to the decluttering process.

If you work from home, having a home office that is both functional and well organized is an absolute must. If you can't find that important proposal for a potential client because it's buried under a mound of paper on a cluttered desk, you're not going to be in business for long.

There are other reasons you should keep your office as organized as possible. You will work better and enjoy more productivity if you work in a clean organized workspace.

Items that don't belong in your home office can be a major distraction that could cause a loss of business and a lot of missed opportunities.

Easy Ways to Organize Your Home Office

Organize Your Files, Then Store

Before you shop for a way to store your important paperwork, sit down and get it all organized.

If you don't have a filing system, now is the time to create one. That means that both your paper files and your computer files should be organized.

The easiest way to handle paper files is to separate them by type such as accounts payable, accounts receivables, business correspondence etc.

Once you've organized everything you can, focus on setting up your storage system to keep your files in order.

You need a storage system that is both functional and easy to access. The type of storage you choose depends on how big or small your home office is, your own preferences and the type of business you're running.

Let's take a look at ideas to point you in the right direction.

Rolling File Bins

Advantus 10-Drawer Rolling Organizer comes with multicolored bins which makes keeping all of your important papers organized and it's an easy system for locating specific paperwork. Since it's portable, you can keep it close to your desk during working hours and move it to an out of the way area of your home office when you're not working. This is a great option to have, for example, if your home office doubles as an extra bedroom or is in another part of your home.

Storage Bins

Simple storage bins placed on a shelving unit is another way to stay organized. There are dozens of options to choose from, but a good choice to consider is the Seville Classics 5-Shelf Home-Style Storage System. It can hold up to 50lbs and has ample room to add storage bins. Locking wheels means it can easily be moved from one side of your office to the other.

Functional Furniture

If your home office is on the small side, clutter can take over pretty quickly due to a lack of usable space. To keep that from happening, you want to go with office furniture that has a lot of drawer space built in. Or go with something non traditional.

For example, a wide table that would normally be used as a dining table gives you lots of space to work, space below to place bins and plenty of space on top for additional bins for incoming and outgoing paperwork and such.

Re-Purpose Items to Keep Your Home Office Organized

Ice cube trays can be used to keep small office items like paper clips, rubber bands and staples neatly organized.

File Management

For files you need to access frequently, try using accordion style file systems. You can place your files alphabetically so you can find them quickly.

Communication

Consider using cordless phones or phones that have blue tooth capability as your office phone. This will allow you to conduct business phone calls from another part of your home when it's more convenient.

Desktop Essentials

The easy way to keep desktop items like scissors, sticky notes, note pads, extra pens and other items handy, is to place them all in a simple basket or plastic bin. This way they are always within an arm's reach without creating unnecessary clutter.

To keep your home office organized, get in the habit of of tidying up at the end of each work day.

Take a few minutes to make sure that all of your paperwork has been dealt with. That means making sure that all of your files have been put away. Organize your desk and make sure that all trash has been removed.

Make this a habit and you'll find the benefits of being organized and controlling clutter will help you be a lot more productive.

Bedroom

Challenges

By design the bedroom quickly becomes the room in a home that is the "catch all" for everything! It doesn't take long before you accumulate more stuff than what you have room for. So the challenge with bedrooms is how to store your belongings and such and still create an environment that promotes restful relaxing sleep.

Solution

Take a look around your bedroom. What you're looking for are ways to use what you already have to create open organized space. Are you getting the best use from your chest of drawers? Is there space underneath your dresser? If so you can use that space to store things like linen. Plastic storage bins and wicker baskets for example are not only decorative but offer great ways to store items.

If your bed has space underneath, there are dozens of storage bins designed specifically for under the bed. You can choose to put whatever you want there. The goal here is to get rid of the clutter that is usually found on dressers and nightstands, for example. Your goal is to find a way to store items so that you can still access them whenever you need to but without them cluttering your environment. I can't stress enough how important it is for you to get in the habit of asking yourself those questions.

"Do I need this perfume that's been sitting here for 6 months unopened?"

"Do I need to hold on to every back issue of People Magazine since 1995?"

"Can I live with 20 pairs of shoes instead of 50?"

Then begin the sorting process.

Best Storage Options

Think about other ways to store items.

You don't have to purchase storage that just takes up more space. You can focus on storage that goes up. Cabinets and shelving units can be just what you need to get everything organized. If you choose this route it's really important to pay attention to how a storage piece will function for you.

You want to make sure that what you choose can hold the items in question but not have so much space that you just end up filling it with many more items, just because you can. That's when storage just becomes a clutter magnet so you need to be careful with the options that you choose.

In the section *"What's Old is New Again - Re-purpose Items to Create Fantastic Storage,"* you'll find some nifty ideas you can use to store items in a nice new way.

Additional Tips

You can get more t-shirts in your drawers by rolling them up. If you find that you have freed up more drawer space, you can store bed linen and other clothing as well.

Bathroom

Challenges

Big or small, there never seems to be quite enough room in the bathroom. Maybe it's because of all of the "extra" items that we seem compelled to place here. I'm amazed by some of the things I've come across in the bathrooms of friends, family and acquaintances.

- Magazine racks or tables
- Stuffed toys
- Litter boxes
- Books
- Complete stereo systems
- Clothing racks
- Beanie Babies
- A scaled replica of the Eiffel Tower (Don't ask!)

There are even some famous actors known for keeping their Oscars in the bathroom!

Let's not forget all of the items in the vanity and medicine cabinets.

Solution

Stick with the program by going through items one by one and placing them in a designated category. Look for items that really have reason to be stored in the bathroom.

Things like shoes, toys, books and too many knick knacks should be stored in bins, donated or sent to the trash.

You can eliminate a lot of unnecessary clutter by allowing your bathroom to function as a bathroom. If you must have reading material, opt for one or two magazines. Hang a simple magazine holder, available at just about any home decor or office supply store.

If you have a lot of hair products causing clutter in the bathroom, you can purchase an inexpensive kitchen drawer silverware organizer. These are great to keep all kinds of hair product items in order. Ideally, you should place it inside of your vanity. Or if your vanity has a drawer, you can obviously place it in there.

If you absolutely must have something like a stereo in your bathroom go with small gadgets that pack a punch. Ipods and any of a dozen other palm sized mp3 players and speakers take up very little space but are powerful enough so that you can "rock out" while you're in the bathroom.

Additional Tips

Use bathroom storage caddies. These are great because they can easily hang on the back of a bathroom door or in the shower from the neck of the shower head.

You can maintain your orderly bathroom by taking a few minutes to tidy up each day. If you see a new clutter problem developing you can nip it in the bud quickly.

Kitchen

Challenges

Kitchens are always the heart of a home. That means that there's always a lot going on in this area of the house.

Meals are prepared, homework gets done here, there's entertaining, socializing and just hanging out. It all happens in the kitchen. Plus thanks to modern technology, many kitchens are now equipped with appliances that are even able to log on to the Internet. Who knew refrigerators had such busy social lives!

All kinds of miscellaneous clutter like mail, school books, every toy your child has, the family pet, clothing and more all seem to make their permanent resting place somewhere in the kitchen.

After awhile all of that clutter seems normal and no one really wants to deal with it anyway. Let's not forget the areas of the kitchen where a lot of organization is always needed.

They are:

- Kitchen cabinets/pantry
- Kitchen drawers

Solution

The same system you learned about earlier applies in the kitchen probably more than any other place in your home. Mainly because of the items you traditionally find and use everyday like pots, pans, food storage containers, various foods, glassware, dish sets etc.

So if your kitchen cupboards are out of control, start with organizing all of your dishes, pots, pans and utensils. Make sure that all of your plates are stacked neatly according to size.

Line up your glassware according to type. For example, wine glasses should be kept on a different shelf, if space permits, from regular everyday drinking glasses.

Pots, Pans & Food Storage Containers

You can reclaim valuable space by stacking your pots and pans. You can do the same with food storage containers. Stack same size containers together and store their tops underneath the individual stacks. That way you'll never have to waste time looking for the right size top for any food container.

Kitchen Drawers

Dump everything out and go through each item.

If you keep grocery receipts, gather them all and place them in a designated folder marked receipts. You could also purchase a small scanner like the Easy Scanner by Neat. It will categorize them automatically so that you can refer back to them at anytime via your computer. This will eliminate paper clutter.

If you keep warranties in your kitchen drawer, place them in a folder also.

If your drawer is full of odd buttons, rubber bands and miscellaneous items, you can either throw it all out or find a jar to put them in. Keep in mind that if you do decide to keep things like that around, you're just moving the clutter from one place and giving it a home somewhere else in your house. So ask yourself if you really need those old buttons.

Infomercial Appliance Wars

If you have more than one "revolutionary appliance" as seen on TV, raise your hand! You're not alone. I've ordered a few myself. It's so easy to end up with 4 or 5 of these magic appliances and then they just end up cluttering the counter top. Plus there's the traditional appliances spread out on the counter as well. It may be tough, but you need to be brutally honest with yourself.

"Do you use any of them on a regular basis?"

"Which appliance is capable of doing more than one thing?

"Do you really need the hamburger stuffy thingy?"

In this case, don't throw out an appliance that works. Keep the ones you use regularly and consider giving away, selling or donating the remaining appliances.

Additional Tips

You can use food storage containers to organize the food in your refrigerator. Opt for the clear plastic ones so that you can see what's inside. It will make it much easier to organize your food to your liking.

Garage

Challenges

It's funny. Garages were built primarily to house a car to keep it safe and out of harms way during bad weather. But if you look at 10 random garages you may find everything but the family car is being stored here. Garages make it so easy to get the clutter party started! In any typical garage, you might find the following:

- Holiday decorations for the last 10 years
- Bicycles
- Toys
- Boxes filled with whatever you can fill them with
- Tools

You name it and if there's room, it's probably in the garage.

Solution

The cool thing about garages is that they do make great places to store things. If you take the time to do it right, you can store everything including your car in your garage.

The main focus should be on eliminating anything you don't need. This is where throwing things away is going to be really important. You have to clear out all of the old items that's been in there since you purchased your home.

If you haven't touched it or used it in a year, then chances are you never will, so get rid of it.

Storage Options

Purchase a Galvanized Steel Pegboard from your local hardware store or online. Pegboards can easily be attached to a garage wall.You can then place your tools on the board and they will hang just fine, thanks to magnets.

For heavier tools like power drills, I suggest investing in a tool cabinet with a key lock. They come with ample shelves for heavier tools. If you have children in the home, you won't have to worry about curious little ones hurting themselves because you can lock dangerous tools away.

Peg boards can be hung high enough so that they are out of reach for small children. The other advantage of using peg boards is that they don't take up valuable floor space.

To reclaim more floor space after you've organized and gotten rid of the items you no longer need, you can consider adding an overhead storage system. You can find these at stores like Home Depot or online at Amazon.com.

They come in various shapes and sizes and can hold varying amounts of weight. They are installed on the ceiling of your garage.

It can be a great place to store seasonal items like portable swimming pools, artificial Christmas trees and decorations, winter clothing, sports equipment and more. You can hang bicycles and canoes from overhead storage units.

They are easy to install and retrieve your items. Perhaps the best thing about using this kind of storage, is that it allows you to park your car in the garage if that's been an issue.

Additional Tips

Use tool storage racks to hold brooms, rakes and shovels.

Floor based bicycle racks are also a great way to gain floor space.

Closets

Challenges

Closets are supposed to be the place where everything is organized and neatly arranged. That's hardly ever the case. It seems we go out of our way to stuff everything we can into the closet!

Between clothing, shoes, gadgets, storage bins, luggage and a long list of other items, to say that closets need a major overhaul is an understatement.

Closets are so important that an otherwise wonderful home can sit on the housing market for months if it has little closet space.

Having a bigger closet isn't necessarily the solution either, especially if you just add more stuff to it. There are closet organizers who make a substantial living clearing out and organizing closets.

Solution

The solution is organization. Even the smallest closets can work quite well if you take the time to organize them properly. Luckily there is no shortage of storage bins, shelves, and wall units made specifically for closets that are available to help you tame your closet clutter.

The easiest solutions are closet organization systems. You can find them in home decor stores, home improvement stores and of course online. These systems are easy to install and have lots of space and shelves. They give you an additional space that goes beyond just hanging your clothes. You can place shoes, linen and other items that you choose to store here in your closets.

Organizing Your Closet

Once you go through the process of weeding out what goes to the trash, what you keep and what you will donate, there's one more step that will be a big time saver the next time you're looking for something specific to wear.

Consider organizing your clothes based on seasons. Summer clothes in one section, then winter, etc. You could take it one step further and organize based on style. After 5 vs casual wear for example. In each section, you could place all of your sweaters for that season together. Hopefully you get the idea.

Shoes can also be stored in a closet organizer. You can also go with an over the door shoe rack. You won't take up floor space and you'll have easy access to your shoes. Be sure to organize your shoes too. Place dress shoes in one section, casual and sportswear in another.

Walk-In Closets

You can also purchase inexpensive purse racks and special racks to hold your jewelry.

If you're lucky to have a really big walk-in closet, there are more great options available to you. One great option would be a storage island. You can place one in your walk-in and store more delicate items there. Place your jewelery rack on top. Store your watches and things like cuff links safely in one of many drawers. Place ties and socks in drawers too.

You can also use closet organizers that are bigger with even more shelving options.

Kid's Room

Keeping a kid's room organized isn't as difficult as you might think. You just need the right set of storage items to make it work. Assuming you've already taken the step to sort everything accordingly, it's time to find appropriate storage items. This same goes for playrooms.

Let's take a look at ideas for a child's room first and later specific solutions for a playroom.

Kid's Room

The Closet

The same rules you follow to organize your own closet should be the similar for a child's closet. Rearrange clothing so that everything is easy to find. You can use a shoe rack to keep shoes organized or use an ordinary milk crate to hold shoes. Make good use of closet shelves. You can organize linen and store it on a closet shelf also.

Storage

Toy Organizers

One of the best ways to keep toys organized is to use toy organizer carts. They come in a wide variety of sizes. They are brightly colored and sturdy. Often they are made of wood with plenty of shelves that have removable bins that are deep enough to store a wide variety of toys.

Toy Chests

The old tried and true toy chests are still a great way to keep toys organized. You'll find simple chests that resemble foot lockers to more elaborate ones in the shape of race cars.

Additional Storage Options

To store clothing and shoes, simple plastic bins with air tight tops are the best options. Especially if you store them in a garage or basement where dampness can ruin clothing if stored in a traditional cardboard box.

If you prefer cardboard boxes, be sure to store clothing and shoes in vacuum sealed bags. You can find them just about anywhere. You need to use a vacuum cleaner hose to remove excess air after you place the clothing inside. Once the air is removed it forms a tight bond around the clothing almost like shrink wrapping. It will prevent air and bugs from getting inside. Vacuum bags also keep clothing from getting moldy in a damp environment.

Organizing a Playroom

Storage & Tables

When it comes to choosing storage to keep toys from taking over the room, look for options that can be multi-functional. This means going with items that can be used for sitting and storage when possible, especially if the child's playroom is small.

Rolling Toy Carts

Rolling toy carts double as toys and when playtime is over, you can pile toys inside and roll it into a corner or closet if you prefer to keep it out of sight.

Closet Organizers

Use closet organizers to store items you may need at any given moment. You can store extra clothing in case of accidents, wash cloths, bottled water and even tightly sealed snacks. Extra items like coloring books, stickers and diapers can also be stored.

If a child's playroom does not have a closet, you can place wire frame shelf units against the wall and use clear plastic bins to store crayons, puzzles, blocks and other toys. You'll save space and having everything in clear bins will allow you to find whatever you're looking for quickly.

Another solution for playrooms without closets is to pick up hooks used to hold hanging plants from the ceiling. Then purchase nylon storage drawers. They are collapsible and very light. Hang one from a hook. You can't store heavy items inside but they are great for boxes of crayons, paper and other light craft items.

Video Games

If your child has educational DVD games, you can either buy storage bins made specifically to hold DVDs or re-purpose items you already have. Shoe boxes work well. No need to buy expensive storage for games. Look around your home for items you can re-purpose to store them away neatly.

Bed Storage

Don't forget about hidden storage space. If there is space underneath a bed you can use that valuable area for just about anything. There are also beds with built in drawers where toys can be stored.

Re-purpose Ideas

Curtains

If you want to hide storage areas, use a regular window curtain mounted on your wall with a curtain rod.

Shoe Organizer

You can take a shoe organizer and either attach it to a wall or get one made specifically to fit on the back of a door.
Then use the shoe slots to store stuffed toys.

Milk Crates

Milk crates can be used to store toys, pillows, linens and pretty much anything else you need access to in a playroom. You can place them on a shelf and tape a sheet of paper on the part of the crate facing you. You can then use that sheet as a label to identify the contents.

What's Old is New Again! - Re-Purpose Items to Create Fantastic Storage

Chances are that while you were deciding which items to keep or get rid of, you may have run across some items you haven't used in a number of years but you don't want to part with them.

Now that you're beginning to enjoy a more organized home, some of those items may be useful by re-purposing them.

Basically, you're going to use items meant for one thing and use them to store items to maintain your newly organized space.

Let's take a look at a few examples to give you some ideas.

Old Luggage

Place an old piece of luggage on top of an armless stool and it becomes a quirky end table. Here's another twist. If you have an old carry on luggage bag you can add a couple of wooden planks to the inside to form shelves. Mount it to your bathroom wall. Add a mirror on the front and you end up with a fun little medicine cabinet.

Lunch boxes

Use fun lunch boxes to store small items like soaps and shampoos or as a place for small tools when you need to do quick repairs.

Milk Crates

Use milk crates placed on shelving units or wooden planks to neatly store items.

Old Free Standing Coat Racks

You can use an old coat rack in your bedroom to hang belts, ties, keys and of course your coat.

Toilet Paper Rolls

Those cardboard rolls can be useful when you run out of toilet paper. They are a simple way to tame electric cords and keep them all organized.

Old Cork Boards

If you have a cork board laying around, mount it on a wall and add some push pins. You can hang jewelery from them and organize it in any way that you want. This idea is usually a big hit with young teenagers.

Library Card Catalogs

If you should happen to find one of those old library catalogs that were used to categorize books, you can re-purpose it nicely and use it to store bottles of wine in each drawer as just one example of what you could do with such a cool piece of furniture.

See What You Can Re-purpose

Use these examples to start looking for way you can re-purpose different items that will also help you keep your home organized and clutter free. You'll be surprise with what you come up with.

What to Do With Everything That You've Decided to Get Rid Of

When you make the decision to organize your home, you will end up with a lot of items that you no longer want to keep, but throwing them in the trash is not a good option either.

Here are some different ways that you can pass on the items that you no longer want.

1- Donate to Charity

There are plenty of charities that are always in need of household items. You could contact the Salvation Army to arrange a donation. Another great place is your local Good Will store. They have stores across the country and are always grateful to receive used but good quality goods. Everything from clothing to home furniture, books and home decor items can be donated. Battered women's shelters are also in great need of clothing, food and toys for children.

2 - Garage Sale

People love garage sales. It's fun and often they find items they would have never found anywhere else. A garage sale also allows you to make some extra cash.

3 - Sell Online

Craigslist and Ebay are popular choices for selling items online. Just be mindful of scam artists and don't send any items until you are paid by a local buyer. Ignore any inquiries to your ad suggesting that you send the item and they will pay you after they receive it. Only deal with local buyers and never meet with anyone alone.

4 - Family & Friends

Let family and friends know that you are organizing your home and getting rid of some items. Invite them over to see if there's anything they would like to have.

Have fun with this!

Final Thoughts

I hope that reading this has helped you to think about ideas and action steps that you can take to start improving your life in all of these different areas.

If you've enjoyed this book, I'd really appreciate it if you would take a moment to leave an honest review.

I'd love to hear from you and I welcome your comments as I love to put a name to those who are serious about creating change in their lives.

Good luck and I wish you the very best success!

Jessica

Now Available in Audio

"The Pursuit of Self Improvement" series is now available in audio!

Visit the author page to listen to free samples:
http://www.amazon.com/author/jessicamarks

Enjoy!

Legal Notices and Disclaimers: